# FLIP

———

NORMAN DEL ROSARIO

BESPOKE STORYTELLING

*Gerardo. In your career, you've saved lives. In life, you save mine everyday. God assigned you to me and you perform your duty with effortless commitment. I cannot imagine or conceive what loneliness is knowing we are truly brothers in spirit. Your parents did well. Y finalmente, Gato-beesh.*

# CONTENTS

# 1

## HOOD NINJITSU

### FALL 1982

My penance began because I'm alive in place of someone who isn't.

Fog saturated with ocean salt floats to the last corner of San Francisco. It dissolves in the back of my throat, and I gulp. Hold your right thumb up. That's the overhead map of San Francisco. True north is the top of your nail where the Golden Gate Bridge protrudes and connects to Marin County. That lower right bend where the nail and skin meet is Visitacion Valley. My 'hood. My incubator.

When blocked on the sidewalk with, "Where you from?" I never claimed "Sunnydale" because I'm one bus stop out of the projects. Before they were lower-income housing, the Sunnydale projects were transitional housing for returning World War II veterans. Repeating rows of rectangular box units evolved into a convenient place to shelve the lower socio-economic populous: the Black and the Brown.

This new emergence of open-air corner crack cocaine sales led to drive-by shootings from rival dealers. Whether it was the CIA or the drug cartels who brought dope in didn't matter. Sunnydale, or the "Swamp," was the epicenter of crack sales. Shootings, up close and personal stabbings and prostitution were byproducts of that business.

Reggie and I found pockets of laughter while riding the city bus home despite being surrounded by imminent gang fistfights and corner D-boys ready to pull triggers at the slightest look of disrespect. We had a brief window of time to balance our arms out like surfers in the middle of the bus aisle. "Touch a pole for balance and you're gay," became the childhood challenge from point A to B. I just wanted to avoid static shocks from touching a pole. I'd get shocked touching the spiral thingy on the spine of a notebook, the metallic eraser fastener on a number two pencil and a metal bolt on a bench. Even brushing up against people, I'd get pricked by a static pop. Clapping my hand, stomping my feet and then slapping the thing I wanted to touch would ground me and usually prevent these electric bridges.

My Olympian balance emerged from negotiating a side-winding bus up and down the hills and sharp turns on the San Francisco grid.

Just two adolescent boys cracking up at fat people, short people, smelly people, dirty people, old ass people on the bus switched to stoic vigilance once we entered Swamp territory.

The corner liquor store was the last turn before we got off and had to sprint to Reggie's front door. Before we got off, we had one last laugh at the landmark graffiti on the side of the store, which had been there for all of sixth, seventh and now our eighth and final grade before high school. In unison, we rapped the spray-painted words, "Dirty Hoes don't get chose," and busted the fuck up. That wasn't the zinger. Right above it was a rushed spray painting of a girl's face with bangs, a bob haircut and three straight line strokes for lashes for each eye. Over her thick lips was an outline of dick and balls.

But next to that was, "F I L P S will DIE." It was supposed to read "FLIPS," a derogatory term for Filipinos. It carries the same hate as "Nigger," "Chink" and "Spic." It was a warning for other Filipinos. Reggie thought I was Puerto Rican or some flavor of dark-skinned Mexican until he heard me speaking pidgin Tagalog or "Taglish" to my family.

Weeks earlier, a Filipino drunk driver crashed into this graffiti'd wall. Moments after the collision, a gathering mob discovered a child from the neighborhood was crushed and killed instantly. During the news coverage of the suspect's arraignment, I couldn't tell what ethnicity he was due to the beating he took before the cops saved him. I knew he was Filipino because the whispers that reached me said it was "so and so's" cousin — a tactical reason to tuck my chin and hide my face.

On another unfortunate day in the 'hood, a white dude on a bike strolled through the Swamp at an "enjoying Golden Gate Park" pace. That fool got dog-piled and then rained on by D-boy fists with the quickness. I used that commotion as a diversion to slide by undetected.

Race out of place was an automatic robbery or beat down. Non-residents needed an escort like I did. I had a limited day-by-day Ghetto Pass to and from Reggie's family's government-assisted apartment. Along the way, I knew Samoan David enough to give an up nod and a "Wassup, fool." Michael, my older brother, was homies with Terrance, Drew and Dre, who lived between Reggie's place and mine at different checkpoints. When they saw me, they threw a peace sign to validate my pass to anyone who may have been targeting me.

When we made it from the bus and inside Reggie's, we

were safe as long as we stayed away from the windows. We'd be on the floor the whole time anyway, propped up on our elbows and sifting through crates of comics. Side-by-side. Not talking. Handing each other the comics we just finished.

Stillness and silence is the gateway to astral projection into two-dimensional comic book pages. It's not a fourth-wall audience perspective. I'm an invisible observer standing inside the panels. I'm standing beside fine ass curvy chicks who look like they are modeled after Raquel Welch or Marilyn Monroe. I hadn't hit puberty but that shit was coming. My eyes traced the silhouettes of the X-Men's Phoenix and Storm. Comics actually showed an exposed hairless vagina! Reading in the prone position kept my boner wedged in place. I couldn't believe artists got away with it. Shirtless, ripped men had their belly buttons exposed. When women were drawn in two-piece bikinis, their privates were right smack dab in the middle of their stomachs for the world to see. Or, so I thought. Until I realized girls have belly buttons, too. And their reproductive organs are in the same pelvic region as boys.

Eczema wouldn't survive in Wolverine's body. His mutant healing factor would identify and neutralize imbalances in the immune system. Repeatedly reading X-Men was like reciting the Rosary. Devoted focus and whispering dialogue would activate my Mutant "X" gene and remove eczema that covered my eyes like a raccoon mask. It was only a matter of deep and sincere repetition.

Reggie was embarrassed he lived in the projects. I was embarrassed about my dry-ass reptilian face. I could be the first Filipino with vitiligo. But none of that mattered on the floor. We read in solitude. Oblivious to time and space and the Crack War.

When the streetlights came on, the worry of catching a

stray bullet from opposing gangs returned to top priority. We slid the comics back in their plastic bags, then peeked out the window like side-by-side periscopes to see if there was a bus rounding the corner that I could catch. If not, I had to book it back home on foot. When I chose to run, one notch below an all-out sprint while controlling my wheezing was a maintainable lifesaving pace.

Sometimes, a random pack of loose pit bulls would gallop in my direction. Easy fix. Cross the street blocks before they see or smell me, keep your attention ahead at the horizon, breathe sllloooooow so you don't give off a fear scent and, most tactically, use parked cars as visual shields, and you can avoid becoming a dog chew toy.

Use the same strategy with nearing dope dealers. Again, cross the street blocks before. As you near them, orient your body completely away with your back to them. Fake an up nod to absolutely no one in the distance. This accomplishes the following: one, they'll assume and associate that nod with you knowing someone in the area. Two, it signals you're not a customer or rival seller. Lastly, I was a tiny brown kid who, at a glance, was either Mexican or Samoan or Tongan. Either way, race in place. Ghetto Pass verified.

I'm the founding grandmaster of 'Hood Ninjitsu. But you can't teach this.

As soon as I made it to home base, I kicked off my shoes at the base of the stairs and dropped that heavy ass backpack with homework I'd never get to. My older brother and sister were busy with after-school activities because that's what academic excellence looks like. Mom worked the night shift as a labor and delivery nurse. My Dad would be the first one home, but not until afternoon cartoons wrapped up.

I B-lined to my Dad's chair upstairs that overlooked the

street. At dusk, the sun reflected off the window so I could see out, but day shift workers, dragging their feet home, were blinded. The upholstery of his chair was silky, smooth-lined corduroy. Rocking back and forth while raking my fingers along the grooves, I recharged my spent mind. My life force power bar redlined after losing energy from proximity to classmates, teachers and people on the bus. Rote learning and bible study further depleted any reserves I had. I'm that marathon runner that collapses at the finish line.

I had a window where no one would slap my hand away from scratching my eyelids. My index and thumbnail were precision tweezers to peel miniature sheets of dead skin off my eyelids. The skin would first get raw, then flaky like dead shed snakeskin. I'd feel for a loose corner on a flake of slightly raised dead skin and ... ahhhhh ... peel.

Eczema was a perpetual cycle of inflammation, raised and raw, to flaky pastry-like stuff. The moment someone flinched at my eyes set off a series of likely scenarios. Girls would play it off out of pity, but more than enough times, bullies noticed and stated the obvious.

"What's that shit on your face?" replays because an older kid at school said it in a full library. Seeing an opening, his sidekick blurted, "It looks like dried mango."

The city bus stopped down the street, and Dad broke through the curtain of the afternoon fog. A red glow swinging like a pendulum from his hand would give away that he was taking a quick drag of a Lucky Strike cigarette, unfiltered – his favorite.

A traditional greeting of an elder would be reaching for their hand and guiding it to your forehead. As the back of their hand contacts your forehead, "Máno Pó" is the proper request for a blessing from the eons of ancestors reaching you in the form of your parent or respected elder.

My father was cool with "Hi, Dad" from the top of the stairs.

He headed straight to his room for the decompression ritual. He wiggled into a sauna suit, which is basically a garbage bag with holes for the head and elastics to choke your neck, wrists and waist. Swinging punches in extreme heat is what I later learned to be a form of stress inoculation. Make training suck so when you're in actual combat, it's easy. Real training begins after a long workday and when you've wrung out all of your physical energy. The standard has been set.

I returned to rocking in his chair and surveilling the street from above. I dreaded my brother and sister coming home, asking if I did my homework or noticing fresh blood on my eyelid and stating the obvious, "It's not gonna get better if you keep scratching." I found temporary peace in my aloneness. Temporary, because no one is truly ever left alone. I never felt lonely. In fact, in aloneness, I feel whole and held. If I kept still long enough, a trap door beneath me would drop open, and I could freefall into daydreaming. Predictable oncoming conversations made me want to back into corners like my Dad's chair.

The Geneva Drive-In Theatre was an immediate left, then right turn from my block. Backed-up traffic and brake lights signaled a movie was about to start. Drivers funneled through the ticket booths where the cashier would count heads and charge accordingly. For those who wanted to save money for popcorn and drinks, smuggling passengers in the trunk was the way to go. The groups that decided to smuggle pulled over, popped their trunks and as one lively party initiated, "Chinese Breakfast!" The driver and passengers spilled out and changed seats, with two, sometimes three, jumping in the trunk. Always two or more. Never one. One time, I saw a boy and a girl get in, and she guided his hand underneath her shirt and let him cup her tit. A girl would never let me do that. I wanted to feel tits and "do it," but the precursor to that is having a friend circle that included girls. You need a car and places you'd want to be. That wasn't a future I wanted, so nix the resultant sex. Plus, girls got grossed out just making eye contact with me.

While I rocked, peeled and watched the streets, cartoons played in the background.

Boom! Dad's fists would embed into the canvas-covered heavy bag. "Right-hand hospital. Left hook cemetery." That's the intent of each punch. After each punch, the loose chain the bag hung from would flail, "Ka-ching!"

Dad moved like a two-page flip animation. On page one, he coiled like a cornered rattlesnake. Flip the page, and the bag is bent in half, his body extended like a shot putter's follow-through.

Boom! Ka-ching! Dad was earthquake-strong. Knowing someone trying to harm me would have to confront my Dad made me able to savor my solitude in the shadows.

Middle school is a slideshow of flashing snapshots. Balance on the bus. Laugh at a drunkard's artwork on the side of a liquor store. Read comics. Run for your life back home. Rock and peel to cartoons. The percussion of Dad obliterating the heavy bag. Except that last night of the final Geneva Drive-In movie.

Traffic backed up. People smuggled themselves, and the line of cars inched into the parking lot in their designated spots, and ... that was it. The drive-in scene would go out of business because this new technology called VHS and Betamax movie rentals eliminated the need to drive to drive-ins or theaters. Why watch a movie now when you can see it a year later in the comfort of your own home?

The fog morphed into a cloud canopy over the valley. Sheets of fog would break off and look like stretched-out pieces of cotton. They would glide down the street, indicating the direction of the wind.

I was rocking and peeling while Dad beat the heavy bag beneath me. Boom! Ka-ching! It must've been daylight savings because the streetlights came on while the cartoons continued their run, and it was already dark. A muscle car's exhaust idled at a low rumble sounding like, "potato potato potato."

Smog vapors coughing from the tailpipes shot up my nose. The car must be right in front of the house. I lean over and look down at a car parked facing the Drive-In. They're late, and the doors don't fly open. A breath later, the driver's door with a rusty hinge creaks wide open. His dumbass is gonna have his door taken off by a drive-by car flying up or down the street. He's not from here. The passenger doors remain shut. A greasy, stringy-haired white dude gets out of the driver's seat wearing foldable flea market reflective sunglasses. I can see the hinge on the bridge. At night. From where I sit upstairs, separated by a window, I can smell the stench from his armpits. His neck is sticky from sweating all day. Just as I transport into comic books, "I" float, descend and transport my "awareness" to the street. He walks to the trunk and pushes the key into the lock. As the key goes deeper into the lock, it activates each driving pin, making a succession of muffled clicks. The streetlight above the car casts an orange hue.

The trunk squeaks open. A little white boy who could be my classmate, other than being white, is in the trunk. He didn't climb in. He was already in there. The driver sifts through garbage around the kid's body. The white boy's lips are mouthing something, whispering. The people who tried jumping in the trunk to save money crouched in a fetal position and always laughed. This kid was flat on his back. His eyes tracked the driver's movements. The driver seems to ignore the kid by working around him, lifting a cloth, and moving a hammer from one side of the trunk to the other. There are tears welled up in this kid's eyes. But his face has no expression. His mouth hangs open.

My eyes dart throughout the trunk when I see his wrists bound with an extension cord. His head flops toward my house.

The driver lifts his arm and puts his hand on the trunk, ready to close it.

The kid looks at me.

He sees me and I see him.

The stinky white dude's head starts to tilt upward to me.

I thrust my head deep into the backrest of my Dad's chair. The back cushion envelops my head, and I hear my irregular heartbeat struggle to find rhythm. I dig my palms into the armrest and push myself deeper into the chair.

The trunk shuts.

I catch a whiff of Lucky Strike smoke.

I brush off the mound of dead eye skin and blow off any remnants I collected from my eyes. I run to my room and shrink to action figure size in the dark.

"Anák! Do you want to eat?" says Dad, still winded.

"Yes, Dad!"

Leftover Chicken Adobo sizzled, and the aroma encouraged me out of my room. My Dad asked as he walked into the bathroom to rinse off from his workout, "Kamusta ka ná, Negrito?"

"Good, Dad," I mumbled with a mouthful of food. I

could do to him what I did to everyone else: misdirect, hide in plain sight, conceal my horror. That was the standard length of my conversations with him, so I could check off that interaction for the night and not worry he would ask about what I just saw.

The days that followed repeated the same pattern. Reggie's, home, sleep, school. I went through the motions with an even deeper apathy for the futility of school. Small people were in danger. I was in danger. Carefree kids wouldn't be so carefree if they knew danger lurks beyond the fence, between school and the front door to their house.

In Catholic schools, you exercise penance through repetition of the Rosary. Each bead is a prayer. A Hail Mary. The Lord's Prayer. The transitional "Glory Be…"

Confession is one of the Roman Catholic Sacraments or religious rituals imparting divine grace. Periodically, you're ordered to go and confess that you cursed at your parents behind their back or you looked at a ripped-out page of a "Playboy" … some shit like that. The Priest would prescribe a menu of prayers, sometimes two Hail Mary's and one Lord's Prayer, for penance. At the conclusion of those prayers your slate is clear to sin again.

When I saw that kidnapped white boy's face on a missing person panel on the side of a milk carton a week later, I felt his soul had already left this plane. An infinite recitation of the Lord's Prayer would never remove the fault I embedded in my heart. I didn't yell for my Dad that this kid was taking his last breath. I didn't bang on the window to intervene in this kid's murder.

A little over a decade after this, I'd be nose to nose with Dad on his deathbed, in that moment right before the spirit leaves the body. His organs shutting down. No will or electricity can prevent each of his cells from the inescapable death process.

Just like that little white boy.

I was THE LAST FACE he saw before he died.

A boy just like him looking down from above.

"Will anyone know I'm gone?" was the last thought I heard from his eyes.

I will.

"You will ..." he responded before the trunk closed.

I'm alive in place of someone who isn't. I earned this penance. However long it takes to work off my cowardice or until it's my turn to die.

## 2

## WHAT'S MY NAME?

### SPRING 1987

The Integral Yoga Institute lives atop one of the many hills in San Francisco. The building was a multi-roomed Victorian style house and looked like it had been built by two different architects who didn't know each other. The left is a cylinder with an inverted cone on top. The right is stacked blocks with a triangle roof.

To not disturb the serene vibe inside, I ripped open my Velcro wallet with Michael Jackson's peeling image on the front just outside the entrance. The receptionist at the front desk hole-punched the "Om" symbol through my library card-sized class pass. Om, pronounced "Ah-oohh-mm," written in Sanskrit, looks like a "3" with squiggly protrusions. The initial syllable, "Ah," represents birth, the breaking of the silence. The deep "oohhh" represents filling one's life with events, and the final "Mmm" is the cessation of that life cycle. The fourth component of the practice is the silence before the repetition. The song of birth, life and death. Dawn, noon, dusk and night. Spring, summer, fall, winter. Om.

The scent of incense saturates the carpet.

The living room was converted into a quaint boutique gift shop. The bookshelves house the Bhagavad Gita, Upanishads and esoteric booklets on astral projection and Tantric sex (hand-drawn genitalia).

A once new but now yellowed and wrinkled poster of the Sun Salutation sequence is pinned to the wall. The male practitioner has armpit hair and is dressed in a onesie while executing the poses. I could smell his funk through the photos. A quick tuck job could have eliminated the outline of his dick that distracted from his perfect form.

I blame the photographer.

Yoga practitioners came in twos. I paced the boutique to avoid small talk before class. The double takes in my direction told me they couldn't place me. Was I a high schooler, maybe the son of a yoga student or employee?

The class was in the attic. The stairs were pre-building code steep, so you had to bring your knee to your chest to climb them. Walking into the attic, you needed to tilt your head toward the center of the room to avoid the angled beams that converged at the apex of the ceiling.

Once in my spot, I learned you scan the room, and when you make eye contact, you offer a polite down nod with a subtle smile. I could do that because once I did, I was free to lose myself within myself. My wheelhouse and what I came here for.

Yoga class was my treat for dropping Dad off at physical therapy. He suffered a predictable heart attack due to his greasy, artery-clogging, fried Filipino diet. On top of that, he lifted hundreds of cigarettes to his lips over his lifetime to inhale noxious gas. That nicotine and soot altered the molecular structure of his organs from vibrant life fibers to waxy and sick decaying meat. On the ride to and from appointments, his heart valve would audibly "click" with each heartbeat. Surgeons took a vein from his leg and ghetto-rigged it to his heart. The Doctor said the warranty would only last "a couple years, if that." The ease at which these words rolled off his tongue told me he had said this hundreds of times before.

After I dropped Dad at home, I negotiated some time to drive and do my own thing. Legally, an adult had to be with me as I drove, but he was too tired and just grateful that I sacrificed hanging out with my friends. I was petite and had to reach wide like a bus driver to control the steering wheel. I'm surprised the cops didn't pull me over.

A dusty independent bookstore, a comic book shop, that seedy-ass boxing gym in the Tenderloin and this Ashram were my new corner couches. Guaranteed places of uninterrupted solitude while hiding in plain sight. No peer would find me here.

The instructor dimmed the lights. This was late 1980s yoga before the watered-down flows, designer outfits, mats with print and the business model that students leave euphoric after a tidy 50-minute class. Here, when in standing bow pose, it wasn't enough to visually hit it. There were no mirrors, and this was decades before the selfie, so I first developed an inward awareness. Physicality is the entry point to the practice. The instructor demanded perfect posture and exact balance points. Remember, this was a practice. Not a gym membership to get a pump. Involuntary trembling indicated the beginning, not the completion, of the discipline.

"Where is your gaze? Where are you directing your breath energy?"

As the instructor paced in an oval she'd admonish occasionally, "Just because you think I take my eyes off you doesn't give you permission to ease up and lose focus."

Out of my periphery, some students either fell out of balance or released the pose out of fatigue. Even in dim light, I saw eyeballs dart to me, noting I was the last man standing. Then they'd re-focus to right themselves.

My ability to stay in physical and mental discomfort with my mouth shut was penance payment. My life is now one big act of contrition and attrition. In early boxing, a referee would chalk a line on the ground between two pugilists. The fight would continue as long as the fighters could put their toe on the line. I didn't come to yoga to get high. I came to toe the line over and over, find my brink in impossible postures and face whatever was coming for me.

Dad shrank as I grew. The heavy bag didn't get any rest. Despite my initial rail-thin outline, my muscles became as dense as concrete. As I hit the bag alone, I heard the garage door open behind me. It was him, and he'd repeat shit I already knew, like, "Dig your toe into the ground."

Boxing is not complicated. Once you know the principles, it's a matter of fighting, sparring and drilling. Dad gave me the basics. A smoker telling you not to smoke is a clear message of "what not to be" because of their bad breath, yellow eyes and dry cough. And him giving me technical tweaks on my boxing form came from someone who can no longer perform those moves.

In my head I shot back with, "Shut the fuck up, man." Like the little punk asshole I was because I just fucking knew what I was doing.

And with that, the instructor anticipated me trailing off. "When your mind wanders, simply bring your attention back." I'm back in my body through my breath.

The closing meditation sealed all that swirling energy inside as we concluded class in the corpse pose. This pose is exactly what it sounds like. You're on your back and you look dead. Dusk classes started dark and ended pitch black. The street lights barely angled up toward the ceiling.

The darkness in the studio is safer than the darkness that follows me home. When alone, I see things, I hear things that others can't. Since human souls were around me here, the likelihood of those three glow-in-the-dark entities with big heads, who stood shoulder to shoulder in my room, wouldn't make an appearance. They'd risk being seen by others and that's not what they wanted. Oh, and that chorus of fat men chanting in exaggerated, deep guttural voices in a language I've never heard before wouldn't wake me here. Aliens were in my room. I fucking heard Tibetan Monks chanting from the opposite side of the globe. I have to ward that shit off while serving my sentence. I'm a boy who can't multitask to save my life. I can barely do one thing at a time except yoga. This was the only time I felt safe from the things that others immediately ignored or were invisible to them. Crowds and loud noises scared away the energies that wanted my attention. It's only when I'm alone that weird shit happens to me. In this space, I'm not whispered to, shaken or startled.

It wasn't until decades later I learned about the introversion and extroversion spectrum. The way I understand their differences is like a battery recharging. Extroversion from loud conversations in bars and introversion from closing the shades for an afternoon nap. When heads turned in my direction, cringe and irritation arose while I anticipated scripted conversations. "Do you have a girlfriend? What are you going to major in college? I'd rather be daydreaming, drawing or reading because that's my gateway to what I can only describe to you as an unpopulated Narnia. Solitude. Alone. Not lonely. But that's the catch. Be alone and be haunted.

People in proximity keep the whispers and annoying spirits from approaching me. Now, I have to figure out how to be among people but not have them talk to me.

The instructor orders, "Observe your breathing."

She knows my mind was taking the off-ramp.

Naturally, my exhalations drew out further and further, and inhalations filled my entire torso with the same pace as the ebb and flow of the tide on the shore.

Observe breathing.

Eyes closed. Darkness. I imagined the illumination of the streetlight on the roof.

I'm deaf now.

No.

The instructor's knees creaked as she sat cross-legged near the door.

I don't hear others breathing. They're controlling their breath. This isn't naptime at daycare. We're all still awake.

"Bring your awareness inside."

I can do that.

The inside of my eyelids becomes a dome. No light seeps through. No after images of silhouettes from other students or the light from the window lasts in this blackness.

Black.

"Bring your awareness inside. Observe your breathing." She didn't say that. I did because she's spacing out these directives. I know what to do. She's allowing us to plummet into ourselves.

In this dome, random plumes of invisible indigo appear and then evaporate.

Wait. I see endless space. I envision a curtain, a wall, a boundary at the furthest point. I'm placing those references to gauge the distance I'm seeing. The problem is what I'm seeing is infinite black. There's no horizon or hard distant vantage point.

I might be stationary. However, I am weightless, like a stray balloon tumbling in the sky. I'm looking for a reference to where I am. In this space, there is no up or down.

Oh no.

I'm not fucking breathing. I haven't taken a breath in … How long haven't I been breathing?

Then it dawns on me. I have no body in this space, and there is no time. That observer behind your eyes. I'm that. There's no muffled sound. There are no sound vibrations because there is no receiving structure. No ear. This is not a womb. Even before I was born I heard my family speaking to me and placing their hands on my mom's stomach.

I am NO WHERE.

This is NO WHEN.

Alone.

Still.

Floating.

An ocean breeze and sun warming your face are pleasurable sensations interpreted by the brain, and we call that peace. I am this consciousness hovering in THIS space. This is peace. Absolute nothing. As the masters describe, this is the silence between thoughts. Decades later, I'd read about Dark Matter. The theorized binding undetectable stuff holding celestial bodies together. This was that.

Here, there is no looking forward to. No memory of what came before because there is no past or future. Only this constant renewing present moment.

"Oooooooommmmmmm."

It's coming from a distance.

I hear it!

This person's eyes are closed. Their eyes are shut. Hold on. This is a first-person point of view.

There's a person chanting, "Om." It's the teacher. How do I know that?

I.

I'm laying flat on my back on this carpet. I'm this person with their eyes closed.

"Slowly, come back and at your own pace. Gently, open your eyes..."

I do that. There's just one problem.

Who. The. Fuck. Am I?

How did I get to this ... information floods back.

My name is Norman del Rosario.

Next question. Where am I? As the lights turn on, I remember I'm in a yoga class. In San Francisco. In a Victorian attic. Spooky but cool as hell. I'll worry about where I parked when I leave this building. Or, did I take the bus?

As we exit the attic, I remember it's proper etiquette to nod and say, "Thank you."

I'm walking behind this Filipino kid, Norman, and his head is on a swivel.

I'm confused. With each blink I see a kid named Norman. And the next blink I see what he sees.

I shake my head and I'm back in myself.

Me. Negrito.

I'm back inside the car, checking the back seat and locking the doors. All souls, entities, angels, and demons reside on this plane of existence. They see me, and I see them, but now I know we're all here simultaneously. For some odd reason, the veil has been lifted for me and for the rest of my life, I'd never figure out why. The curious use Ouija boards and attend seances to access the vision I have.

I've always understood, "Be careful what you wish for..." But, I didn't wish for this.

I don't go to yoga, meditate or do Tai Chi to escape. As French philosopher Friedrich Nietzsche warned, "If you gaze long enough into the abyss, the abyss gazes also into you." I do this to stare back. And, maybe, teenagers shouldn't be reading about morbid dudes like that. But I did.

They, the spirits, can't jump-scare me if I see them coming. I stay ready so I don't have to get ready.

I failed to save that little white boy. Flashes of images reveal to me he was beaten, sodomized, defiled and had his bones broken before he was dismembered and buried in pieces. That fate is intended for me, and dark forces wait for their window to maul me. When that happens I won't be running.

Even before I saw him get kidnapped, entities wanted to lure me by myself. When my mom was late to pick me up from kindergarten, and I stood in the pickup line after school, the crowd of kids dwindled as parents slowed their cars to a stop and their car doors flung open. My classmates happily leapt into their cars and drove off one by one. One car screeched from a side street and didn't align with the program. The car cut the line, stopped in front of me and the passenger door flung open. The driver leaned over the passenger seat, which had candy spilled all over it. As he waved at me to enter the car, my body unplugged from my power source, and I was motionless. The demon contorting his face to smile failed to mask his eyes, lusting with the desire to bludgeon me.

My tears frightened him off.

Moments later, safely in the car with my mom, I didn't have the words to connect. I felt her concern for me as I refused to look at her, holding my terror to myself and staring out the window. As she put it, almost 20 years after that incident, "You didn't start talking until you became a police officer."

She giggled and in her Filipino accent she added, "You were my autistic one."

I never told her or anyone about the kidnap attempt on me. Asking for help would endanger anyone who tried to protect me. These were the seeds of despair, and that's how *they* methodically wear you down, and would eventually try to take my life.

On the ride home, I traced the undulating telephone wires with my eyes. Up and down and up and down all the way home with my index finger in sync and writing a continuous "U."

# 3

# LONG ISLAND ICED TEA

## WINTER 1990

Two Taco Bell bean and cheese burritos and one hard shell taco with two mild sauces was my go-to meal to dine on the hood of my buddy's car as we watched airplanes take off and land at the San Francisco International Airport. Our designated gravel strip was off a shoulder of road parallel to the 101 Freeway. The violent rumble of the airplane engines felt like it could rip our clothes off if we were just inside the chain link fence. The explosive energy emitting from the engines distorted the air around them, creating waves with the accompanying roar. Because of Doppler, the earth-quaking turbulence seemed to originate from the empty space behind the plane as it picked up speed on the runway.

When we had our fill of plane exhaust and when the Bay Area frigid night air became unbearable, we ventured into the airport. In those days, the airport was either packed with stampedes of people deplaning or boarding or eerily hollow.

Victor, the ringleader, held ideas that didn't require

much money, like tonight or going to the cemetery to walk along open plots, explore caves at Ocean Beach or cruise the Tenderloin spotting nearly naked prostitutes.

In the airport, we'd compete in foot races and challenge each other to hurdle over the stanchions and break dance to no music on the slick floors. The corridors seemed like a mile long. I could spot security guards rounding the furthest corner just by looking up and fixating at the furthest point. While the boys were being loud and unaware, I'd be the one to alert them with "Chill." After a back and forth of, "Why? We're not doing anything wrong. We ain't hurtin' nobody." The security guard would happen upon us, a tame group of teenagers having an unremarkable conversation, and we'd be on our way to the garage to race left behind luggage carts.

Predictable is preventable. We'd get kicked out if we were loud, obnoxious and disrespectful. So, don't be that around authority, and we will get to hang out at SFO. I could never fully immerse in their fun because I was the only one looking out for danger. And the only one just looking out.

One thing on our airport checklist was to sit at a tactical location with a clear and unobstructed view of the arriving passengers. Fine-ass girls travel, so we were positioned ready to gawk. My buddies would lose interest, get fidgety and get up and go if no females passed by. Every passenger had a face worthy of examination and absorption. I was able to look at faces when they weren't looking at me. I was like an anthropologist behind the trees because they were oblivious to a tiny teenager off to the side. Some couples would run toward each other in the meeting area, collide, embrace and kiss. At that moment, they were in their world of two, with the airport dematerializing around them. Would anyone feel that emptiness in their chest for me? And the sight and touch of me would be the only thing to fill their cup. Nothing mattered to them, and I want nothing to matter to me.

In reverse, two enmeshed souls reluctantly tore apart when they said goodbye. The poetry I had read up to that point shed light on the love I thought I wanted when I processed it from the neck up. Something primal overrode reason. Only symbiosis with a woman would satiate this hunger. If I had someone to protect and fuck maybe the world would dissolve around me, too. Instead, I'm not worthy of protection. I'm not deserving of a girlfriend. I stepped out into the open when I failed to take that little white boy's place. Whatever bullet or knife's trajectory is predestined to end me can't be sidestepped. I'm vigilant but not avoiding my imminent end. I just don't want to be blindsided. I want to collide face first to whatever's trying to take me out.

Pick-up basketball runs broke up the airport, beach tunnels and cemetery rotation. The locations varied based on who had a friend of a friend who had keys to a gym after school hours. One run ended up at a school in the hippie Haight Ashbury district. Plumes of weed smoke coalesced with fog rolling in from the Pacific Ocean. As we waited for the guy with the keys, dudes who were invited to run would bounce balls with their backs to the street, joking, unaware of hungry homeless people and *hypes* high off heroin, shuffling and stumbling behind them. Yeah, I didn't like these new guys.

The rumble of a gas-guzzling muscle car broke the silence down the street. Muscle cars made of metal had American souls, versus the plastic "Rice Rockets" every Asian kid flaunted. A Mustang rounded the corner, the driver a Filipino dude with a flat top. He paid a pretty penny for fat tires, rims and an even coat of paint. He was eyeballing for parking spots as soon as he rounded the corner. He catches my eyes looking at him from an entire San Francisco block.

Someone mentions, "There goes, Marcus."

Marcus. The guy that's been slow rolling on the block for the last 10 seconds, and you're just now noticing?

"He's an Oakland cop." Victor adds.

All heads turn to Marcus. He steps out, "Good evening, boys." Victor introduces me, "Marcus, this is Norm. He wants to be a cop." This was before I learned to use my voice to begin the back-and-forth of social pleasantries. I had a deliberately weak handshake to gauge a man's need to assert his perceived dominance. He was tall for a Filipino. Zero fresh off the boat accent. No hint of pronunciation from growing up in a household where he heard or spoke Tagalog. He had a twang. Not a growing up in the hood southern twang. This was a serving in the military adopted "country" conservative twang. He had long fingers. Manicured. He had the latest Jordans. His Mustang felt "off the rack," and I got the impression he didn't turn a single wrench.

While shaking his hand and feeling his grip, his body had "air" or "space" in it. I felt it through his palm and forearm. Every inch of my body was packed tightly, built from the inside out. Hardness is achieved from self-inflicted pain, and I could gauge someone's tolerance just by laying eyes on them. He was in shape but not to the level I expected a street cop to be.

We funneled in the gym, warmed up and picked teams. I had one move. Drive to the basket. When the ball touched my hands, I tracked my defender's descending eyelids as he was about to complete a blink. When his eyes were almost shut, I'd explode forward in a controlled fall toward the basket. When my defender opened his eyes, he had to twist his torso to see the back of my head. I was already beyond his outstretched fingertips.

When I jumped I heard, "Damn" from below me.

It was like I was in a foot race in a gym filled with sluggish children half my size. They weren't small. I'm usually the shortest in a group. Their reaction times and top speeds felt sedated. Except for Marcus. He moved like them, but he was tactical. He knew where the ball would bounce after hitting the rim and he'd be in position to catch it. He'd use his teammates as pillars to move around and block a chasing defender. A pick. When he shot the ball, he lifted his arms smoothly, not fast, then flicked his wrist, sending the ball floating in the path of a perfect rainbow parabola. His shooting finger aligned with where the ball would drop through the net.

I was an explosion waiting for detonation. He was finesse.

After the games, Victor went his way, and Marcus offered me a ride home.

"You don't mind cruising?" he asked.

"Sure" was probably my first word to him. Even when we got introduced, I just nodded.

Other night cruisers revved their engines, provoking him to race. Eventually, they gave up as Marcus inched along at green lights. Taxis and other drivers on the road honked from behind and then drove around us even though we were in the slow lane.

As we approached the Tenderloin, he looked at me out of the corner of his eye when I elbow-checked my door lock and rolled my window halfway down. Almost annoyed, he asked, "Why'd you do that?"

I still need to hear the streets. A man whistling to target this Mustang to carjack would be a good time to punch it to turn at the nearest intersection. A prostitute trying to open up the door and get in wouldn't have success. Plus, I need to cool off from basketball but not catch pneumonia. When I became a Field Training Officer years later, I imparted that your senses are a radar dish to street stimulus. Marcus wasn't annoyed. He was impressed.

Shrugging in response to questions like these felt like the most efficient way of communication. But, I still had to learn to voice what went through my mind. That's how people communicate. They talk. A lot. Most of the time, it's nothing worthy of breaking peaceful silence.

But didn't my behavior tell everything about what was going through my mind?

"Wanna grab a drink?" he proposed.

"Sure." Probably the second thing I said to him.

My bloodstream and pores felt depleted and dry. He parked in front of a club with a line formed in front. The beefy security guards waved Marcus in. I wasn't even voting age at this time, but since I was with Marcus, no one checked my ID.

Drum and Bass, House and Techno warred with each other from different rooms in this building. I stumbled like I was stepping in potholes from the vibrations disrupting the balance in my inner ear. I looked drunk before I was. He leaned on the bar and commanded, "Order a drink." I never consumed alcohol and didn't know the name of one drink other than "beer." I felt his irritation for my indecisiveness as I stared and glanced at other people's drinks. "Alright, pussy, you get a girl drink."

He grabbed his drink and disappeared into the crowd.

The bartender pushed a thin cylindrical glass in front of me. "It's a Long Island Iced Tea."

I felt like I was going into kidney failure from not drinking water all day and then playing ball. I downed the drink and my upper lip pulsated to my heartbeat. My feet dangled off the barstool. Beneath my eczema, which was fading now, I had a baby face. I looked like an abandoned child in a sweat suit at some underground club in the seedy part of San Francisco.

Marcus ended up pelvis to pelvis with a girl he couldn't reach his arms around. They were gyrating and the visceral fat around her midsection molded around Marcus's concealed gun in his waistband. They were cracking up in each other's faces, drunk as fuck, bouncing to House Beats. On the other hand, I held onto the bar for stabilization even though I was sitting.

A cute girl with curly hair sitting across from me sipped the same drink I had. The bartender spared me the umbrella, but the color of the liquid and glass were the same. She smiled, winked and used her tongue to move the straw toward her mouth. I moved like a sloth twisting, looking over both of my shoulders to see what the hell she was looking at. I didn't want to fall out of my chair even though I was secured in place, like a kid in a barber chair. She was alone. Her silhouette wasn't touching anyone else's. My deodorant had to have worn off hours ago. If she gets near me she's smelling my ripeness. She's still looking in my direction. I have $20 in my pocket. Random, but not. Not enough to buy her nothing. Her white collared shirt is buttoned down to the middle of her sternum. This alcohol in my bloodstream is distorting time. It's helping to muffle the music. I can see the appeal of these effects that people don't usually have access to.

Marcus snaps his fingers in front of my face. "Hey, loser. Want another drink?" I swipe my fingers across my neck. "Yeah, you look more retarded than you did earlier." I rack focus over his shoulder, and that curly-haired girl still looks at me.

He orders another drink, and while he waits, he proudly shares, "Did you see me getting down with that fat chick? We looked like the number "10" dancing together."

I crack up, but still hold onto the bar with two hands.

I see it.

Marcus is "1" and his dance partner is "0."

The girl looking at me said, "Come over and talk to me." I hear it in my head. Her mouth didn't move. She pivots in her chair while still maintaining eye contact with me. Her midsection is exposed, and her skin is as light as her egg-shelled colored shirt.

There's an ice cream sandwich called Neapolitan, with chocolate, vanilla and strawberry sections. My body against her body would be like where the chocolate and vanilla meet. "You're innocent, but not." She adds speaking directly to the observer behind my eyes. This dive bar is teaming with weed and dope dealers, shoulder to shoulder with regular dudes who punch a clock from 9 to 5 and save their cash to splurge at places like this. This was my first sausage fest. I can't figure out why she honed in and missile-locked on me.

She doesn't have any visible tattoos. Her face isn't fatigued for an early twenty-something from this area. How the hell did she get here? She wants my attention. Why? These D-boys have fucking rolls of cash in their pockets; the worker bees just cashed their checks. I look like a child with dried vertical salt streaks on his face. Everybody has money and income. I don't. If I had a voice, I'd ask her, "Why me?"

but my unbroken stare carried these thoughts through her eyes and into her brain. My suspicion of her interest overrode my instinct to look away.

She was perfect.

Inevitably, towering men invaded her space, and her mouth moved to occupy their minds while she stayed transfixed on me. The last thought I sent her was, "Something's not right." Decades later, she still appears inhumanly perfect. Ageless. Sent to seduce me. Take me off course. Soothe, soften and pleasure me away from...something else I'm supposed to do.

"Let's take off and eat." Marcus had his fill of dry-humping with random women. I looked back at that demon, and she magnetized a crowd of D-boys and mindless career clock watchers.

I placed one foot in front of the other back to his car. I blinked and awoke in a 24-hour diner.

Marcus, mid-bite into a cheeseburger, mumbled, "You'd make a good cop, but you got one problem."

One? I'll take it.

"You don't talk, dude. Being a cop, you're convincing, Jedi-mind tricking and asking the who, what, when, where, how and why. You just look at people like a weirdo. Look. I get it. You're observant. But there's no job for just being observant. It's awkward, bro. Start talking."

If he thinks my silence is awkward, wait till I talk. I talk more than anyone I know ... in my head. You just don't hear this constant chatter. But, I guess I gotta start talking if I want a job. I nodded. I added, "I hear what you said. You're right."

I sensed he knew he drew me out in the open where I didn't like to be.

So, he changed the subject.

"You know that kid who got kidnapped who was all over the news a couple years ago?"

Marcus is a cop so he has the inside info to stuff like this. He's sworn to protect kids and hurt kidnappers and molesters. I want to do that. "He went to that school we just played at."

...

He went to that school we just played at.

...

He added, "You know that kid is fucking dead. There are sick fucks out there, Norm. Dangerous motherfuckers, too. Can you wrap your mind around that shit?"

I slow nodded, controlling the impulse to punch the glass window and cut my hand to divert my anguish to the pain in my lacerated hand.

I startled Marcus when I responded, "I did think about it."

"The kid?"

I lied with, "No."

I had to access words and put them on deck.

Scrabble!

That's what talking is like for me. I piece together letters into words. Only when it's complete can I manually place them on the game board and say it out loud. It's always been a tremendous chore for me...and a game I don't like playing.

Back to Marcus, once those words were locked and loaded in my mind, I thought, "Do I put these thoughts out there?"

He tuned into me for the first time of the night and didn't have a quick comeback.

I let it fly. "There's nothing else I want to be. Predatory behavior can't be lobotomized from criminals but someone has to stop them. You say I can die or get killed in the line of duty. I say that's the cost of doing business. Bring it."

He paused. Looked at me and came back with, "I don't know if anything you just said was some kind of speech or if that was even English, but it sounds like you're committed."

I laugh at him laughing at me.

I warned you I'm awkward.

# 4

## POWER EXCHANGE

### SPRING 1995

This homeless guy with a ratty beard bordering on dreadlock density stares past me. It was like he was fixated on a single point across Market Street. He was mumbling something. I believe, based on his concentration, that he was oblivious to his pants dropping around his ankles and his hand stroking his semi-erect penis. He was two people in one. Both are unaware of the other. The top half mentally checked out, perhaps astrally projecting himself walking across the street, and the lower half soothing himself underneath a bus shelter.

This is the Tenderloin, the other sliver of the San Francisco grid where the remaining populous of crackheads, prostitutes and D-boys run wild in plain sight right in front of the police. Watch your step for uncapped used needles.

My hands are already wrapped systematically and taut. The obstacle course from the train to the front door of Newman's boxing gym is my warm up.

Head on a swivel. Chin down. I'm pinballing from one sidewalk to the other. Perpetual jaywalking. Hoodie draped over my eyes. My pace says, "I need a rock," so I'm ignoring whistles and avoiding eye contact with the D-boys who spotted me from a few lights away. Crackheads smoke rock in closed business doorways, and Tricks stick their asses out while leaning into cars giving their menu and negotiating price.

I step over a guy smoking crack right in front of the gym. He pivots on his hip like he's gonna rip a fart to give me space to walk past him. He's polite, "My bad, champ." Once inside, funk from fighters who don't use deodorant punches up into your nose. Percussion from boxers digging into the heavy bags collides with the dribble dribble dribble of the speed bags. It sounds like marching band warm-ups.

Two guys are sparring in the elevated ring.

In between their punches, "Come at me, nigga." and "Get some, bitch."

If you're ringside watching, don't be surprised when one of them leans over and invites you with, "Lace 'em up, hoe."

From behind me, "Wanna get some work?"

Wesley King, who has the keys to open and close this pit, makes matchups. These were pre-waiver and license days to run a boxing gym where someone could get killed. Like I said, Mr. King had keys, collected and pocketed 20 bucks from the beginning-ish of the month. He kept track of membership in his head. The windows were taped up with newspaper, so all you could see was the streetlights and sky. Whoever put that now half-ripped "condemned" notice from the City of San Francisco on the front door forgot to collect keys and change the locks.

I wanted work, so I nodded and scanned who he had me paired up with.

This light-skinned dude was lacing up his Air Jordans.

My Chuck Taylor canvas classic had a worn hole in the sole. He had his headphones connected to his CD player and was boppin' his head while rapping ... Damn, I can't make out the song. He just checked his pager. Great. He's either a pimp or D-boy from around the corner with aspirations to box. Or, he's keeping his hands sharp for his trade. There were more fistfights than shootings back in those days.

We step into the ring. His eyebrows are slightly above mine. That means his reach is at least a finger length longer, maybe. He's top-heavy because he lifts. His shoulders and chest are bulbous and hollow compared to my, at a glance, wiry little boy build. My quads and calves are girthier than his. He's got that prison build, like an inverted triangle. Before the bell rings, he smirks.

When the bell rings, it's like someone ran a red light and T-boned me from the blindside.

I'm not smelling blood. I'm tasting its sweetness at the back of my throat. He charged with straight lefts and straight rights. All landed flush on my nose except the last straight right, which landed on the top of my headgear because I cowered.

Sparring etiquette goes like this. It's the frog in the pot. You turn up the heat slowly. You reach out. Not even that. You extend your arm toward his face. He dodges or slaps your hand. He extends his arm, and you repeat. You're circling either clockwise or counterclockwise. A round is three minutes, and this craft work and "feeling out" round is signaling to your dance partner; this is the level of control I can return to.

The second round in sparring and beyond is the gradual increase in speed and how much mustard you put on a punch. It's agreed upon. You go hard. I go hard. You back off.

I back off. We wanna turn up the heat and mix it up for half a round. We do that.

Not tonight. This dude launched out the cannon straight at me. My bad. Protect yourself at all times.

You fight how you live. He was aggressive, big, straight at you. A visual intimidator.

He had success with a straight punch attack, so he tried it again.

I planted my lead toe, the one closest to him, and used that as an anchor to spin away from him. Think matador and a bull.

You fight how you live. He invested everything in that initial barrage because he expects people to fold in his life. Bullies are punk bitches once you punch them in the face. He fights like he knows that, and he's making me his bitch. Back-and-forth street fights are rare because you see people who believe in themselves literally fighting for it.

I don't extend my hand to his face because it's the first round. I joust his fucking jaw with a left jab. A term in boxing called "Keep him honest" means make him pay for being open. I gotta keep this dude honest or he's gonna think I'm giving him my consent to beat my ass.

His ferocity is real. He uses it daily to keep order on his block around the corner.

I also want to come back to this gym.

I also don't want him to shoot me when he sees me on the street.

If I beat his ass, he'll want revenge, and get his "get back."

If I take a beating, I'll learn how to take a beating, even though I deserve it for being alive in place of someone who isn't, but I'll give others in the gym consent to do so. What's the use of coming down to the gym?

I lean to the left, then to the right, dodging punches I can read because his eyes light up and he cocks his elbows before he throws. He doesn't know he does this and is perplexed about how he can't touch someone close enough to hug.

I wipe my nose, and there's red blood on my red glove.

Bam. I'm looking up at the light bulbs. He caught me with a punch while I was marveling at my own blood. Now, I'm stepping backward with my gloves covering my face. No gliding footwork to evade. Just plain walking backward.

Wesley King states the obvious, "You gotta do something back, young blood."

Thank you for that wisdom, technical advice and direction.

This isn't a boxing gym with accredited trainers and a progressive curriculum. This is a post-apocalyptic abandoned building where dudes off the street put on gloves to fight.

The bell rings. The round is over.

My sparring partner's nose is flaring. His mouthguard is halfway out his mouth. His eyes are wide because he's hyperventilating and panicking. He doesn't know how to breathe. I'm not being elitist, but I am gatekeeping. I'm not teaching this motherfucker how to do pranayama.

Ding ding. Round 2.

He charges, but his lactic acid saturates his thighs, and he moves like he is lifting each foot out of the mud. He throws heavy arm punches in my direction, and I swat each of them out of mid-air. He barrels me into a corner and I spin out. As I'm moving, he catches me with a clean hook on the top of my head, and I start what's called "stepping in potholes."

I'm not hurt, but he jiggled my central nervous system and disrupted communication to my legs.

Straight punches are coming, so I shell up.

He blew his load. No more punches came. He has zero energy in his tank to throw another punch. I know this, but I'm bouncing to regain my equilibrium.

Update. I landed one punch to his 20 sloppy ones. If he gets another break between rounds, he will come back to kill me. He believes he can because I'm giving him consent by not doing shit.

I dislike him for punching me.

A thought. We're not sparring and working on technique. We're fighting. In a boxing gym.

I get it now.

I have to hurt him.

I take a deep breath and direct oxygen and chi from my lungs to flood my brain and every single artery, vein and nerve ending. The timer counts down from 2:30. There are 30 seconds left.

All I need is the time it takes me to sneeze.

Ahhhhh-

Choo!

That floating rib at the bottom of his rib cage. I cracked it with a left hook. The large intestine begins around the belly button. I javelin a straight right above it hoping to see a piece of shit run down his leg. I launch a left hook at his throat to close his carotid artery so the blood won't go to his brain. If I'm off by a centimeter, I'll hit his jaw and whiplash his neck short circuiting his nervous system, causing him to collapse to earth. A win-win.

I miss his throat and jaw because he was falling forward from the body punches. My left knuckle struck the brow of his headgear. My knuckle compressed the foam in my glove at the moment of impact. It would have been a knuckle against his orbital bone if he wasn't wearing headgear. I would have cracked his skull with my bare hands in a fist-fight. I don't need a bat in a street fight. Check.

He remained hunched over like he was in suspended animation while standing over a water fountain to take a drink.

But, in the real world, he was unconscious while standing up in a boxing gym in the Tenderloin.

If the ring ropes weren't there, he'd fall face forward onto the concrete floor from the height of a dining room table, probably paralyzing him if he landed on his head.

Instead, the ring ropes caught him, stretched and sling-shot him into the center of the ring on his back.

Uh-oh.

Fucking uh-oh.

I pull off my gloves and kneel next to him. I killed him. The train is a mile away. I'm warmed up, loose and coursing with cortisol and adrenaline, so I'll be on the train in a four-minute Bannister mile. No one knows who anybody is here. This was back when there were no security or traffic cameras, so I could've just walked out of the gym and been alright. Plus, this is the Tenderloin. Snitches die in ditches. Nobody would've said shit.

Then the dead sparring partner whispered, "Damn."

He rolled on his side, took a knee and I supported his elbow. He jerked it away and said, "I'm good, blood."

I think "blood" was a remnant of the 1970s scene. We grew up greeting each other, "Wassup, blood." It must be from the bell bottom, jive-talking, disco era.

Fearing he would retaliate later, I tried to pretend to rearrange my nose when I felt him looking at me. I even wiped my nose, pretending there was blood. I walked over to him to give him a fist bump. He was seated when I wanted to let him know he got me, too. "Maaan, you opened up-"

He cut me off. "You got hands. You're good, blood."

When someone from the Hood says you got hands — You got hands.

He knew I wasn't from the streets because I wasn't talking shit. He knew I wasn't a threat to him, outside the ring. He knew I wasn't gonna use this as leverage against him. He knew I was afraid of everybody because I didn't make eye contact with him or anyone else in the gym before or after I dropped him.

After he checked his beeper, he reached for his gym bag. He moved the opening enough for me to see the butt of a gun. He reached in and lifted a wad of cash he had to "C" clamp with his hand.

This guy is a Sergeant in his organization. He's visible on the streets. Doesn't talk shit or doesn't have a knee-jerk reaction to getting touched up. Everybody in the gym avoids him. He's somebody.

He laid the wad of cash closer to me and farther away from him on the bench.

He nodded at me, "You earned this."

Absolutely no one was looking at us.

Even Wesley King found a way to look busy in his staged office.

"What's your name?"

I reached out my hand, "Norman."

He shook his head and had a hearty laugh.

Ah. I get it. I'm stupid. You never give your real name.

After he recovered from laughing he said, "I'm Ghost."

"Because you're a light-skinned black dude, and you got made fun of because you're assumed light and soft." I didn't say any of that. I thought that.

He smiled and said, "You're 'Lefty.'"

"Ah. Because I nearly killed you with left hooks. My Dad told me, 'Left hook cemetery, right-hand hospital.' Fun fact about me, Ghost. My Mom is ambidextrous but mostly left-handed. My sister is left-handed. I was born left-handed, but when my grandparents saw me becoming left-hand dominant and using my left to draw, they'd send Cece to switch the pen to my right hand." I didn't say any of that. I thought that.

He offered me cash and a nickname. No one gets a nickname without being liked. I liked that he liked me. And I liked him. He took his ass beating like a man and didn't have poo poo face toward me.

Then I realized that because I nearly killed him with gloves on, I confirmed I had the strength to seriously harm anyone he pointed out on the street. He liked me enough to visualize me by his side. I was never in a gang although I had some fistfights with gangs. And this was another of many opportunities to join one.

It was an honor to be recruited by someone running a corner. I had a skill and he recognized that.

But I had to leave to make it home, clean up and hang out with Marcus tonight.

I put my hand on the wad of cash and looked at Ghost, "I'm good, brother."

He nodded, "The offer will be there when you want it."

I left. If the cop thing didn't work out, I'd have to support myself somehow. To date, my job skills are fighting, reading and seeing ghosts.

Later that night, Marcus kept me updated on the progress of my application and background to the Oakland Police Department.

I needed to land this cop job.

Marcus picked me up, we cruised, talked and ended up in an unlit parking lot next to a dark ... I couldn't make it out. Apartment? Motel? Hotel?

This abandoned building had a scaffolding exoskeleton and wind-torn plastic whipping in the wind. It wasn't empty. You just had to walk through the front doors to get in. This was once a hotel; the marble floors and columns echoed and amplified every step you took to the front counter.

In the middle of the lobby, where endless couches were once lined, was a lone pool table with people around it. I didn't stare, but I took note out of the corner of my eye. The discoloration on the tiles and dust imprint showed the after-image of the former furniture arrangement on the floor, like the shadow of a human silhouette on the ground after being disintegrated by an atomic bomb.

Marcus, who worked with the Vice unit at times, said prostitutes started using this thing on the computer called the World Wide Web to advertise their services. This was one of those meet up spots. This was part of my pre-academy training to study how the underbelly of society behaves. And this place also has live sex shows.

The one dude around the pool table was dressed just like me. A checkered flannel, Ben Davis work pants and Doc Martens boots. I'm through and through a neighborhood Frisco Kid, and my thrift exuded a conscious step back to let the needy gather attention. He, most likely, shopped at the Army Surplus store like I did. There are two on Mission Street. This guy was older and dirtier but was surrounded by bony Vietnamese girls with tight bodysuits with spaghetti straps. In between drags, he set his lit cigarette dangling off the edge of the pool table. Burn marks on each side gave away his routine, and this is his hangout. This dude thought he was fucking cat's meow with these girls following him around the table as he hit balls by himself. While he took a hit from his filtered cigarette, I looked away before he looked at me. He had yellow can opener teeth and his neck had a thin film of the day's sweat. If he caught me looking, he'd say something stupid like, "What are you looking at?" Then I would've had to have corkscrewed straight to his chest and knock the wind out of him.

We had to sign in to go upstairs.

What?!

Marcus showed his ID and actually used a functioning pen with ink! Then he signed a clipboard.

Dude.

I'm not saying I'm more street smart than a cop, but that's called evidence you were here for the sole purpose of looking at naked girls.

My turn to sign in.

I showed my ID with my index finger over my license number and middle finger over my address. I felt like a nervous, up-close amateur card magician.

I signed below his actual signature with "wjidsog-pdhfskd."

We walk up a wide spiral staircase and enter a small and nearly pitch-black banquet hall. The only light coming in is from a single open door across the hall. Once my eyes adjusted, the perimeter of this dark room was lined with girls who looked like the ones around the downstairs pool table. Faint light from the open door illuminates their faces momentarily enough for me to determine they're young like me. One of these girls straddles this fat, white, balding white guy. The top of his head is bone bald and he looks like he asked for the "bird's nest" when he went to the barber. They are kissing like it's prom night and no adults are around.

I caught another face. Confirmed young. Collagen-filled

cheeks like mine. No bags underneath the eyes. Protruding clavicles and a flat chest like mine. Like mine... Like mine... Because these are actually fucking dudes.

At that moment, a hand cups then grips my balls from behind.

I override the flinch instinct to pivot in place and spin my elbow to the ball grabber's temple. The voice in my head explained, "If you do that, you'll be fighting with 100 wiry boys, and one or 20 of these fools has a knife." Marcus is packing heat, he'll open fire, and we'll have a crime scene with hella victims, and I'll have to disclose this debacle on my application to the Oakland Police Department."

I focus and go toward the light, putting one foot in front of the other. I walk like a cowboy with stiff boots who has to take a shit. While my ball grabber matches my steps, I catch a glimpse of that fat friar monk looking loser and wonder, "Does he even know?"

In the light, I quicken my step, break the grip on my testicles and keep on walking. Head and eyes forward. Marcus is cracking up behind me. Making eye contact with Marcus and admonishing him, "This stays with us" makes him bend at the waist and laugh in pain.

Time to go up a floor.

The Black Floor. The ceiling, walls and floor were painted black. In the middle of the room, there's a chain-link fence. Within the fence are evenly spaced tables. Overhead lights focus on the tables, leaving the outside perimeter in the shadows.

A man sits with his butt at the edge of the only table in use. I sidestep to look between the shoulders of other perverts, watching what I'm about to watch. The man on the table is leaning back, spread eagle and his legs are in gynecology stirrups. A woman, looking like someone's aunt who never got married, inserts a dildo... No, it was a molding of a fist and forearm. Well, yeah. A dildo. A dildo doesn't always have to look like a penis. Anyway, her level of concentration and focus reminded me of a lab technician mixing compounds to avoid an explosion. She methodically inserted it into his back door. I didn't see it from my angle, but the dildo wasn't going anywhere else.

On the opposite side of the cage, from behind a pillar, I saw a creepy nerd with glasses staring at me. Easy fix. I side-stepped out of his view but made a mental note where the glasses guy stood so I could track him.

Marcus and I were over this floor so we ventured up.

There was a small bedroom built in the middle of another ballroom. I assumed it was a bedroom because it had a doorway and four walls, but no ceiling. It looked like an unused television sitcom set on the weekend. This room didn't have windows, but slits at varying heights. One guy squatted to peer through a low slit. Another lay on his side for the mouse point of view. Two guys stood cheek to cheek to stare through a mailbox size opening. On one side there was an open vent as high as I could reach. The shuffling behind me were guys standing on chairs trying to get a top down angle.

The Green Apple bookstore on Clement Street in the Richmond District is inside a converted Victorian-style house. Former bedrooms are now sections for Esoteric Religion, Erotica, Psychology, Photography and the latest best-sellers. Second-floor wooden planks give and creak with each step. One day I'll fall through and land on top of a kid in the children's section. Walls are lined with tribal masks from around the world emitting a protective sphere around the building. I clocked hours, weeks and months in, maybe, what was a walk-in closet a hundred years ago. I was never disturbed in my designated cell lined with a wall of books behind me.

Here, Krishnamurti, the prophesied next world Teacher on par with Jesus and Buddha, educated me through his books. At the turn of the century, the Theosophical Society, influenced by mysticism, metaphysics, Buddhism, Hinduism and the like, educated and groomed him for this massive role. Krishnamurti had a lifelong gig doing Ted talks before there were any.

Then came the reason he's my guy.

In 1929, he quit.

Look within. Not toward a person telling you what to think. There's no paywall or subscription or intermediary to the truth. No authority. His proof? Think of world leaders – religious, political, philosophical or otherwise. Now look at your newsfeed. Violence in the form of wars and crimes are the rule. Peace isn't around the corner. Idolize no man. C'mon. Do you believe shading in a bubble on the ballot for your favorite pick will highlight and delete violence and replace it with an era of peace?

If Green Apple were open I'd rather be there than in this cheap ass sex walk-through gallery.

Books are my friends. We have the best free-flowing conversations. We don't talk over each other. And I come out smarter. I'm blanketed with hundreds of years of combined wisdom and knowledge.

But, there's no career for this pondering.

The last time I was in the bookstore, someone accidentally meandered and happened upon me in my hiding spot. I was cross-legged with a book in my lap. I didn't flinch when they flinched because that would've multiplied the jump scare by a factor of two. Instead, I smiled softly through my eyes to save them from embarrassment.

A transparent woman, a three-dimensional hologram made of haze, took a step back, turned and disappeared — not around the corner, just disappeared.

I just scared off a ghost.

I'd rather be there passing my time in books, but I just got hired by the Oakland Police Department.

# 5

## SHIT SHOW

### SPRING 1997

M y very first call at the Oakland Police Department was a home security alarm going off. I parked down the block and we approached on foot. I sidestepped up the driveway, checking the front door and side windows, when a Rottweiler rounded the corner from the backyard. He had a clear runway toward me. It took him a few steps to gain speed because he was dense and had to haul all that muscle. His slobber and snorting signaled I was fucked.

My Field Training Officer recalled, "Dude, you were mid-air with your gun aimed at its head!" My body automatically leapt the width of the driveway without me knowing. Before I pressed the trigger, my FTO kicked the dog's ribs, and it scurried away just as the owner of the house exited.

My FTO told the owner, "Your alarm is going off."

"Yeah." The homeowner saw his dog scamper back into the house while I was huffing and puffing with my gun drawn. Our Sergeant showed up and raised his eyebrow at my FTO wondering why I had my gun out on my first call. I holstered my Glock and my FTO told Sarge, "The rookie wanted an early lunch." Maybe implying Filipinos eat dogs. Maybe not. They laughed and I joined in with, "I guess I'll have to wait." The Sergeant nodded at me, gave me a thumbs up and said, "Have fun, kid," before he drove off.

Later that night, I heard the high-pitched whistling emergency alert tone for the first time. The Dispatcher broadcast, "Coming in reports of a stabbing. Suspect seen fleeing the area."

Here.

We.

Go.

My FTO grabbed the mic with the quickness of a gameshow contestant, and she answered, "3L23, we'll take primary." She glanced at me sideways, "You have to get your cherry popped, eventually."

Primary. Officer Norman del Rosario's first stabbing investigation would turn into a murder investigation within minutes. We pull up. A block away. During this critical approach, she programs me, "Look at people's faces. That'll tell you where the scene is and where the bad guy ran off to."

Fire Department sirens in the distance get louder. Strobing red and blue lights bouncing off buildings relieves me because backup is around the corner. Dispatch adds, "Witnesses say the victim is in front of the apartment complex."

My gun is at the low ready, and my finger is floating, ready to pull the trigger at the sight of a man charging me with a knife. First day. Gun already out twice. I almost discharged my gun on my first call and I'm ready to use deadly force on a murderer in the same shift.

No one's screaming. The residents start to file out into the street. Some occupants of the apartment look out their windows. No one is telling us shit. Snitches die in ditches. The streets are watching. Two street truths. A veteran officer yellow tapes off the front of the apartment building and whispers to me as he passes, "This'll take us to the end of the shift." He's happy.

My FTO scans. "Where the fuck is the victim?"

She and I just checked the entrance of the lobby and the walkway leading up to it.

Blood is on the pavement between the planters. I missed it.

There's a heap, a mass with a duster dress covering it. It's solid, fixed and as inanimate the planters beside it. It's crouched in a fetal position. Arms. Legs. The Victim. The puncture wounds that cover the body from the knife used by the murderer looked like 100 smiling mouths. Each stab was the same size creating a slit exposing red muscle. I holstered my gun and squatted beside the body. I held my hand close to its skin. From my FTO's point of view, I checked the carotid for a pulse. The soul that inhabited this body was gone. This vessel is a lifeless mannequin. The spirit or consciousness was gone before the Dispatcher put out this call. It was gone before the witness picked up the phone and dialed 911. I felt and "saw" her last memory, lifting her arms, defending against the knife attack from the suspect. The victim left this earthly vehicle behind. I pray for her soul.

Where you are now, draw a circle around your feet.

When someone enters your circle with hurtful words or physical aggression without your consent, that's violence. Conversely, when you exit your circle into someone else's circle to harm, manipulate or convince them to adopt your point of view, that's also violence. Therefore, the precursor to any act of violence is trespassing.

Once the ambulance medics pronounced the time of death, the Fire Department draped a tarp over the body, cops took statements, the police technician snapped constant photos, reloaded her 35mm camera every couple minutes and then my FTO grabbed the back of my collar and pulled me back. The victim's blood was oozing down the sidewalk and about to hit my spit shined boots. She continued my on-the-job training, saying, "You have the easiest job." She keyed her mic, "Units at this incident, turn your supplementals to Del Rosario." She turned back to me, "From the time we got the call, we showed up, and she's D.R.T-" I interrupted for clarification, "D.R.T?" She educates me, "Dead right there. But you don't write that." She continued, "Then wrap it up with what everyone else documented. That's all you gotta write. This isn't rocket surgery."

The remainder of the night was spent in the Homicide Investigation office. All the who, what, when, where, how was documented. The "why" would be established by witness statements or, eventually, a suspect confession.

The first responding officer is considered the preliminary investigator. The homicide detectives are the ones that take over the case and see it the rest of the way, from what you initially gather all the way up to trial. Jeremy Patterson was the first detective who held my hand through the daunting task of telling the story of this victim's last moments. Jeremy shuffled around the office, always with a stack of papers in hand. He taps my shoulder as he walks past me, "This is how you look busy." His brow had zero tension and his lips and jaw were relaxed with a soft smile. An airport Hare Krishna face in the Oakland Homicide Investigation office. Oakland continues to be ranked as one of the most violent cities in the United States. You'd think the atmosphere would be more tense. Jeremy tracked each word on my report as if each one was written on its own flashcard. He looks like how I feel when I have that singular focus. But he can smile and talk and work with interruptions and not get flustered. I can't. He looks up, "Great report. Make 'According to witnesses, the suspect and victim were seen having a loud verbal argument with each other' to 'The suspect was arguing with her.'" This shows the initial invasion of the victim's safety and space. We know how the story ends, so it's highlighting the suspect's intent through his behavior.

Jeremy was one smooth cat who had a playboy reputation. He taught homicide investigation in my academy. He imparted his brand of cool by advising us, "Remember your A, B, C's. Always be cool." When he added, "Like the other side of the pillow," he found my face and verified I was smiling.

Oakland averaged two homicides per week during the years I served there.

The Homicide Division was open 25 hours a day, eight days a week. These detectives represented the pinnacle of what an OPD officer aspired to be: a master communicator who can get people who don't want to talk to talk. Period. The majority of dedicated young cops looked up to officers who had the respect of dope dealers, parolees and other wanted felons. That trust demonstrated a uniformed officer could rise above public distrust of the police. Talking to the police is a safety risk for Oakland residents. Remember, snitches die in ditches. A highly skilled officer can navigate those concerns and have a genuine relationship with the public. Despite OPD's violent reputation, most of us, at least the company I kept, valued using honest face-to-face conversation with criminals and citizens alike. Selling dope kills the community, but I understand that's the only option some see. It's also unfortunate that some see violence as the first and only means for conflict resolution. Doesn't make it right, but I understand the limited mentality.

I had the opportunity to pick Jeremy's brain while writing my report. He explained to me, "They put pressure on us to stop shootings and murders. You know who's responsible, Norm? The person holding the gun and pulling the trigger. We know that, but if we say that out loud we're racist and we don't care."

The person holding the gun ...

Even deeper in all of us is the innate, irremovable component in our brains on how we resolve conflict: with aggression and violence. Historical prophets and elected officials haven't helped curb that impulse, and the police are an "after the fact" institution. We're advertised as peace-keepers, but that's on par with religion promising to extract lust and adultery with the threat of damnation. How's that working out for us? The existence of the police doesn't remove a dope dealer's desire to shoot and kill his competition.

I can show up to work for decades, as I have, and people won't stop stealing shit, killers will kill, drunks will choose to drive and crash into and kill people, a coach will find a way to have sex with an underage student and a married cop will have sex with a prostitute.

If there is a higher intelligence running this shit show, she's allowing us to fail. This earth is a fucking petri dish. Everyone's just trying to stay alive en route to their jobs to punch a clock. There is another level of existence on top of this one.

I'm losing contact with it.

I pray from habit:

Our Father who art in Heaven.

Hallowed be thy name.

Thy kingdom come.

Thy will be done.

On earth as it is in Heaven.

Give us this day our daily bread.

And forgive us our trespasses as we forgive those who trespass against us.

And lead us not into temptation, but deliver us from evil. I remember.

That little white boy is dead because of you, Norm. You must shove your face in this shit. He'll never have a job, experience the touch of a woman, be able to feel the breeze of driving with his window open across the Golden Gate Bridge because you let that shit happen. And you will show up to this dumpster fire until you die by a bullet and pay what you owe.

# 6

# BE CAREFUL, FOOL

## SPRING 1998

This is the second casket I've carried. I'm in the same position as the first time. Front right. My grip is slippery because I'm wearing these stupid white gloves. Eyes are on me. It's an honor to carry this burden for his family. The midday sun heats my Class "A" police tunic. Mobility in this getup limits my movement. I'm stiff like the robot in "Lost in Space." Thank God it's only for funerals and promotions.

I learned from Dad's funeral. Lock my carrying arm straight down and focus on the grip. The instinct when carrying something like a dead body in a coffin would be to curl it like a barbell, but you'll burn out quickly. Short, choppy steps are necessary to prevent a slip and fall. You only have to make it from the back of the hearse to the dug-out grave. Clenching the handle for a few steps while the family and the entire police department stare at you only requires short physical exertion. A small price to pay compared to paying the ultimate price.

Losing the first friend you were ever vulnerable with is a whole 'nother level of fucked up.

Emiliano's lifeless body jostling inside this heavy-ass box isn't what's dismantling me. It's seeing his mother, father and brothers in psychic torment. Amputees experience what's called "phantom pain" from the location where the limb was. That pain is chiseled on their faces. If I hadn't cried since Dad died, I can put aside my pain of never having one more conversation with Emiliano.

I spoke to Emiliano last week when I came home early from my patrol shift. I paged him our code to telegraph that I was about to open our front door. He and I never had unexpected guests. In fact, one time, someone knocked on our door, and we both tactically crouched. We mouthed, "Who the fuck...?"

We never answered the door, and to this day, I don't know who that was.

No one gets in our space. No one will disturb our solitude. It takes an introvert to know an introvert. Before we became friends, we were classmates in the Police Academy. We'd do that "dude" thing where we would nod at each other for weeks. You don't get invited into the circle just because time passes.

Emiliano grew up in Tijuana and immigrated to Oakland. One rough 'hood to another rough 'hood. His normal. A normal we smelled on each other.

He perplexed me. I couldn't read him or hear what he was thinking. I didn't talk. He didn't talk. When he took his attention off me, I watched how he watched people. His eyes darted from people's mouths to trace their silhouettes, and he'd note the way they put more weight on one foot. He listened to words where I leapfrogged over them to feel the intent behind them. He absorbed people like I did, but in his own way.

Emiliano talks like a Mexican ventriloquist. His eyes

don't emote, he's monotone and his mustache cloaks his mouth movement.

Months into the academy, he mumbled, "I'mma go grab some tacos." Deciphered: "Do you wanna get some tacos?" This was my tryout. He knew I wouldn't talk or disturb his dinner. Joking around and not keeping your head on a swivel along the streets of Oakland is an invite to get your shit took or get shot.

I drove "Lamont," my 1986 Oldsmobile with a cracked windshield and one functional headlight.

We ate on the hood.

Mid-bite, he paused, and his eyes locked on the horizon line at the furthest traffic light. He was tracking someone headed our way, his body still but his head pivoting imperceptibly.

"Hey, man. Let's bounce ..."

Emiliano's body language told me danger approached before he finished his thought. Lamont's V8 engine roared, and I was in the driver's seat, leaning to unlock the passenger door.

At that precise moment, he fell in love with me.

Back to our last conversation at our apartment. As I opened the door, he was in the prone position with his gun trained at me. Finger on the slide - the side of the gun. Not on the trigger.

He holstered his gun in his waistband and joked, "You ain't catching me slippin'."

Through his involuntary laughing, an expression no one else saw but me, he managed to explain, "If you walked in on me you'd see me looking at questionable material on the web." Now bent over, he added, "I would've had to knock you out with this keyboard."

I busted up because he almost walked in on me a couple of times, clicking on videos that froze our computer. He stopped laughing, and his face flipped to squinting to take in a detail of my face, almost like when people micro-paused noticing but trying not to notice my eczema.

His face softened, "I haven't seen you smile in months."

I rationed all my energy to suppress grief of my Dad's passing and I powered off facial expressions.

He cracked my stoic mask as only he could.

And now he's gone.

And how he died...

Someone tapped me on my shoulder, "You good, man?"

It was good timing and a helpful distraction to keep a lid on this rising tightness in my chest.

How?

How did Emiliano die?

It's a blank screen.

A blank movie screen.

I'm in a lit movie theater in San Francisco, staring at a blank movie screen.

The trailers haven't come on yet.

Victor, my homeboy from high school, repeated, "You good?"

I am good because Emiliano's funeral was only a vision that didn't happen. Yet.

I wiped the moisture from the corner of my eye, "Something's playing out, brother..."

Victor tapped my shoulder with the back of his fist, giving me space to work out what I needed to work out. Victor has seen me "zone out" for years, throughout high school until now. He appreciates smoking a joint while we cruise around San Francisco. Him high off THC, and me daydreaming from highway hypnosis. He knows not to overlay silences with placeholder superficial conversation. That's me and V.

Emiliano is on duty. We have opposite shifts.

I flip open my phone, ready to break the cardinal rule of not calling a cop with stupid shit while they're on duty.

There's only one reason I was carrying his casket.

He's about to die.

I dial his number.

Fuck.

He answers, "Wassup, fool."

3-2-1. That's the time you have to say one sentence — no pauses for dramatic effect.

3. His background is muffled. I see. I imagine he's in a small room with other ... bodies absorbing ambient sound. That's why it's so quiet.

2. He tucks his chin down and away. Yeah. He's around cops.

1. As cool as possible, I casually said, "Be careful, fool."

My voice cracks. The last time he heard my voice crack like this was when Cece, my sister, called me the day before my Dad died. She obeyed the 3-2-1 with, "Come to the hospital..." My voice cracked as I responded, "Tell him to wait for me." Emiliano saw that phone call go down, so he knows when I'm trying to maintain calm but can't. A tell he noted and recorded. And now I'm ordering him to be careful because his life is in danger, and he fucking knows it.

"Alright, man." He hangs up.

I'm shown things. Or, I see things. Short moving images. Vignettes. This began before I saw that kid get kidnapped, but now it's increasing and happening when my eyes are open.

Victor is halfway finished with the popcorn.

I judge him. "Really, bro?"

He justifies it with, "I'm not gonna ask you mid-daydream, fool." Getting mad at me for getting angry at him. He waits for someone else in the theater to look in our direction before he holds a single popcorn to my mouth like I'm a baby.

Bitch.

The lights dim.

Stanley Kubrick's last film, "Eyes Wide Shut," starring Tom Cruise and Nicole Kidman, starts. Cruise plays a doctor with an uncontrollable curiosity about sexual encounters despite being in a marriage. Kidman plays his wife, and she admits to her own sexual fantasies with another man. Kubrick's genius is his holding space for each character to meander and explore their own appetite for sex, real or fantasy.

As a virgin, seeing desire and lust that can't be contained by the ceremony of matrimony, relieves my expectations of my first time. A future date, formal dress at a church and a dinner nobody wants doesn't resolve or cage primal desire. Religious and moral laws punish sex outside prescribed authorized locations, like marriage, but don't acknowledge the innate evolutionary directive to advance the species. I think about this shit.

Kubrick plays that out. You're either repulsed from programmed religious response or a complicit voyeur.

Cruise's character manages to infiltrate an underground sex club. Masks and robes are required.

Glamorous models galore wander the mansion. Are they sex workers? Prostitutes? All Nude. All 10s. Long-limbed. 1990's idyllic mainstream MTV music video vixen perfection also masked, escorting guests from room to room. The walls were lined with masked attendees watching live sex in the middle of the rooms.

That novelty would wear off fast.

I'd rather be doing the sex, not that I knew what that felt like.

Especially not in public. I don't know how I'd feel about my penis out in the open.

I lock my gaze on the nude actresses. One female performer was bouncing on top of a male performer. Obviously, no penetration is seen. Is simulated sex as arousing to women as it is to men?

The audience in the theater holds their breath. Heads locked forward.

They don't look at their dates beside them, risking making awkward eye contact with someone nearby. Some wait for the scene to end. Some people's pupils are at maximum aperture.

Victor taps my shoulder. He must be looking around like me and seeing something noteworthy.

He stares at me like he has critical and profound information.

In a breathy whisper, he stares into my eyes and says, "This isn't 'Star Wars the Phantom Menace.'"

Fuck you, Victor.

Fuck. You.

I snort.

Choke on popcorn.

My only move is to get up and scurry to the exit.

I shoulder-bump the hallway walls like that's going to dissipate and dissolve my giggles. Nope. I hear him laughing to himself like an idiot. Someone shushes him but that only makes it worse. He kicks himself out.

As he rounds the corner with our trash, we both fall to the floor, busting up.

I wouldn't see "Eyes Wide Shut" until it streamed online after I retired from Law Enforcement. I cracked a smile at the sex scene but managed to finish the whole movie. Over 20 years later.

As we walked to our cars in defeat, I offered, "Wanna go for a drink?" Our other buddy owns a bar on Geary near Ocean Beach, where we never pay for drinks. Well, Victor drinks. I ordered a red wine to hold and swirl for the night and, maybe, take one sip because I heard wine in moderation is good for your heart.

"I'mma go chill." That's code for he's gonna smoke weed and drink with his other buddies who bet on illegal, underground bare-knuckle and dog fights. Part of his circle and my circle don't overlap. Respect.

I end up driving the San Francisco grid by myself. North and south on Van Ness. East to west on Market and Geary. I cut over to the Marina Green and funnel onto the Golden Gate Bridge. Crossing the Bridge, that frigid Pacific Ocean air feels like you're standing inside a refrigerator. The suicide railing isn't a thing yet, even though jumpers have always been a thing. Would I see one tonight?

Men shoot themselves in the head. Women shoot themselves in the chest. The pain source. It's an immediate way to stop it. Suicide is an option, but a cowardly one. Are jumpers hoping for that last intervention? Are they not committed? What a dramatic way to go. Are they secretly hoping that they will be spoken about after their death? If so, being tethered to how you're spoken about is part of the problem. Fuck what people think.

I'm finally getting tired enough to get home and maybe fall asleep. I hope.

Once in bed, I toss and turn. My timing is off. I need to come in for a landing when I'm on vapors.

Straight up, I'm scared I'm gonna hear whispers of "Norman" accompanied by my bed shaking.

The ceiling lights up.

It's a "510" area code on my phone.

It's Emiliano.

I answer, "'Sup, fool."

I hear a commotion in his background. He checks in, "Hey, dude. You got a minute?"

He's alive. "For you, 60 seconds."

Emiliano breaks it down. "When you called, I was in the Ice Cream truck." Oakland Police Department's undercover white van. "I was with the SWAT fools, and we were about to roll up on a murder suspect a CI (confidential informant) snitched on. When my phone rang, they got pissed before I let 'em know it was you."

Remember the cardinal rule of calling a cop on duty?

In a tactical operation you never answer your phone. Focus has to be like a cat in front of a mouse hole.

He adds, "So a UC (undercover) who has eyes on the suspect calls the takedown. SWAT activates and converges. What the UC didn't see was that he got into his ride and took off. I'm bringing up the rear while jogging in the street. Norm, this dude floored it. I saw the white's of his eyes and he was gonna make me street pizza."

We laugh. We could laugh. Because we know how this story plays out.

He adds, "Straight up, I'm horizontal like I'm flying toward the end zone and he clips my heel with the front of his car."

We're cracking up over the phone when I hear him lower his voice to gain composure.

"I straight up helicopter and land in the push-up position."

From my heart, I project, "I'm so glad, man."

He wraps it up with, "Norm. It's not that I would've acted any different. I still would'a got the fuck outta dodge. It's the fact you called me the moment before it happened. I hung up with you and they called the swoop. Plus, I was ready. A half-second delay in my reaction, I would'a been ran over. And the GI Joe nerds had nothing to say once they knew it was you."

Patrol Officers, vets and rookies didn't blink an eye when I burned incense in my patrol car at the beginning of every shift. And they didn't blink an eye when Emiliano told them of the time I felt an officer get shot and killed.

On a rare shared day off, we'd watch Michael Mann's crime thriller "Heat," starring Robert De Niro and Al Pacino. We memorized every scene and line, and still, we'd lean forward at the scene where De Niro had the opportunity to escape to freedom with his girlfriend or enact revenge on a gangster who snitched on him. To this day, we believe there might be a different outcome if we watched it just one more time.

I dozed off or trailed off with my eyes open toward the end.

On one field trip during grade school, we went to a planetarium, a dome where they would dim the lights and project the night sky with constellations. While other kids grab assed and screwed around I was transported. That dusk indigo sky after the searing orange sun burned itself out was a dimension that, throughout my life, would be the only plane I'd experience peace within.

On the couch, half there, half elsewhere, I was in a similar darkened dome. IN my head. In my drowsy imagination, I saw a white car speed in front of me and I tracked it, fading into the distance. In this dream dome space, I leaned in the direction the car went and sprinted toward it. I pulled out my gun, which was unusual since I wasn't in uniform, and pointed it at the driver of what I felt was a stolen car. Had to be. Then, in this dome space, gunshots rang out and reverberated off the walls.

I flinched.

Emiliano said, "Falling asleep?"

I described the dome, the car and the shots.

We didn't say another word to each other.

He went to his bedroom, and I went to mine.

We waited for confirmation.

Hours later, he knocked on my door to wake me up. He got paged by someone on duty with tragic news.

OPD dispatch put out an alert of an armed carjacking that just occurred. Marked patrol units flooded the area, but Cliff, an undercover cop in plain clothes, spotted the vehicle. The vehicle crashed and Cliff approached to take the armed suspect driver into custody. As he stood over and was pointing the gun at the suspect, two rookie cops who didn't know Cliff opened fire on him, thinking he was about to execute the guy on the ground. The cops killed Cliff.

I saw it unfold at the exact same time Emiliano and I were sitting on the couch.

Out of curiosity, I asked, "What color was the car?"

Emiliano confirmed, "White."

Norm is quiet. Norm is different. Norm burning incense is Norm being Norm. Norm gets a pass calling people on duty. Norm sees ghosts. That's Norm.

In police tactics, the front door is the fatal funnel. That physical plane is where cops are the most vulnerable. That's why you either commit to staying out or, when you enter, launch yourself in and deal with what you get inside.

I'm perpetually in that doorway. Half of me is here with you. Half is somewhere else. I'm here in front of you, but at any moment, I'm pulled to pay my penance by being in moments of imminent death.

# 7

# KILL THE BURGLAR

## SUMMER 2001

OPD Dispatch sent me on a call of a single shot heard in the area of the Lake. I began the mental checklist of a Patrol Officer who wants to get off his shift on time. It's 3 a.m. My shift ends at 6 a.m. If I find a dead body, God I hope I don't, add six hours from the time I see it. That means I'll be up after being awake for a whole ass day. And that depends on Day Watch hustling out to the scene. They won't.

I slow roll with high beams and both spotlights on. Other than two bundled-up homeless men sleeping on a park bench, there's no one lying flat in the open grass field. No one is running for their dear life. No dead bodies in the bathrooms, either.

I swing back around to check all the "looked for a dead body" boxes and see if the two homeless guys on the bench saw anything. These men can sleep through anything, so all I need is a name and an "I didn't see shit" statement. It's Oakland. Gunshots and helicopters are ambient white noise.

The guy on the right side of the bench is laying sideways

curled up like he's lounging on a couch. His head is on his side of the bench. Moisture from his hot breath billows from his mouth during the freezing early morning. The other guy's sitting on the left side of the bench, but so drunk and passed out that his upper body is hanging over parallel to the ground, draped off the armrest.

Steam seeps from his mouth.

I step heel to toe on the wet grass, trying to avoid a slip and fall down the slope to the bench. As soon as I shine my flashlight, a circular crimson plate below the bent man reflects the light back to me. It's not uncommon for dumpster divers to collect random shit they think is valuable.

And, hold up, he's holding a gun.

And the steam wasn't coming from his mouth. His internal moisture and heat were escaping through the hole in the side of his head. The hole drips blood every few moments, like a garden faucet you didn't fully twist off. That crimson plate is a pool of his coagulated blood.

I'm getting off at 9 a.m.

To confirm death, additional boxes need to be checked. Obviously dead, check. Yes, that's an actual box. Pupils unresponsive to light. I flash my light directly in his eyes. Fixed pupils. Check. Next: no pulse. Fuck that. I'll falsify this police report and say I felt for a carotid pulse and felt nothing.

I tilt my head to match his head tilt. He is perfectly still. A mannequin twitches more than this poor guy. There is no light or life behind his eyes. This guy had enough, pulled the trigger and put a period at the end of his timeline. That's the real report.

Whatever was going on in his head was so incessant and loud that he wanted it to shut up.

I get it.

Once he pulled that trigger, the electricity that animated his body went to hell or, at least that's the collective auto-religious response.

Day Watch patrol officers show up. Homicide Investigators show up. Supervisors show up. I hand over my report to my relief officer. I didn't get a felony arrest during my shift. Only reports. A rookie officer needs to be stocking up the evidence locker with dope and guns. If you're not turning a page in patrol you're just driving for dollars.

Oh, that other homeless guy on the bench? He slept through the whole thing. They GSR'd his hands (tested for gunshot residue), it was negative and he passed a polygraph.

There was, however, gunshot residue on the suspected suicider's gun hand.

My work week is over, but next shift, I'll stop that car rolling four or five deep with its headlights blacked out at night, circling a dope corner. That equals a gun, dope, someone with a warrant or at least a car chase.

On my days off, I'd drive and wander. Since I was making money, I could actually buy books instead of being confined to reading them in a bookstore. Several coffee shops were anchor points throughout San Francisco, like Caffe Trieste in North Beach. Their table tops were inlaid with multi-colored mosaic tiles. I like running my fingers across the bumps and grooves — anything to take my mind off my mind. There's a picture of Francis Ford Coppola hanging on the wall. The barista told me he wrote part of "The Godfather" here.

In old-school encyclopedias, there were sections dedicated to biology. Several pages had transparent overlays, each one illustrating the circulatory system, nervous system, digestive system and major organs. As you turn a page, you see where each system "lines up" with the others.

Visions overlay my field of vision. They play out in front of me. And as I walk and wander or drive the streets of San Francisco, it's inevitable the world underneath this one will reveal itself again and again and again.

On cue, as I'm driving, I see a point of view where "I'm" actually descending into a courtyard of a two-story apartment complex. It's an overlay. Not a split screen. I'm driving, looking through my windshield, but simultaneously, "I" turn to the front door of a second-story unit. The point of view of this "camera" pushes in. It's not my point of view. I'm watching someone else watching. Like I'm standing over some guy's shoulder.

The front door knob is a rusty copper color. The door's locked. A counterclockwise twist confirms that.

This is my sister's apartment and she's on the other side of this door.

This point of view side steps to the sliding kitchen window. It comes into focus. A wooden stick jams the window from opening. My sister is playing defense to this man trying to get in.

It's my day off, and I'm staying at Mom's. Cece's apartment is two freeway exits south of San Francisco.

Should I call her? Is this just a random — No. Images I'm shown are precursors to actual events. What's that phone call gonna be like? "Hey, Cece, lock your doors and the windows because someone is trying to break in and rape you."

This is what I rehearsed.

"Hey, Cece, it's probably nothing, but lock your front door and the sliding kitchen window because I saw someone trying to break in."

Someone is trying to break in. I'm a cop. Why aren't I driving there? How about, "What's your address?" By the time I show up, my path will intersect with the burglar's, and I'll resolve this problem by eliminating the threat. Either by pulling the trigger with a contact shot to his temple or jumping off the second story and using his body to break our fall.

Here's the problem. I'd be driving there with the intent to kill the burglar. That's pre-meditation. On face value, a pervert would just be trying my sister's door handle. Burglary is a property crime. Let me ask you something. When a burglar enters the home of your loved one and they come face-to-face in the dark, does that feel like just a property crime?

In my heart, he's worthy of death because I saw his lack of care for my sister's safety. You see, that makes sense to me. Just twisting the door knob qualified him to be on the receiving end of all of my martial arts techniques until he's not breathing or brain dead, preferably both.

So, I gave her a call and she answered, but didn't say "Hi." Caller ID. She knew it was me.

I break the silence, "Hey ... do me a favor."

Do me a favor. I gave it away. Whatever follows, she'll know it's coming from my daydream state, the one she said I was always in as a kid.

I add, "Lock your front door and the window over your sink."

Silence on the other end.

I ask for confirmation with, "Did you hear me?"

I hear her gulp, and she manages an "Okay."

Bitch. I'm looking out for you. I didn't want to make this phone call in the first damn place. You don't have to answer me like that. I didn't call Cece a bitch to her face because she's fucking gangster. She'll destroy me. Like that one time when we were kids, I hid under her bed to jump-scare her after she got out of the shower. She walked past the bed and I grabbed her leg like a ghost. She stomped on my head with the heel of her foot and kicked me in the ribs as I was trying to get to my feet. Once on my feet she swung haymakers to the back of my head and spine as I stood on one leg. Dad heard the commotion and came over to investigate. I was cowering against the wall and Cece was huffing and puffing from whooping my ass. Naked. Her towel fell. Fucking ghetto ass family fight. Dad giggled, turned around and walked away.

I tell her in my head, "Do I need to recap and fill in the silence with a list of weird shit that tells me that you're in danger?" I'm not trying to write an essay on how these visions spell out danger for people.

Just last night, I was dispatched to a case involving a missing person. When I got there, hella asians were standing in front of the given address. The guy who called, the uncle, looked at my name tag and started speaking English, not Cambodian, Laotian, Thai or whatever his language was.

"My niece hasn't called us."

I'm immediately irritated. Someone not calling you back doesn't mean missing.

He added, "They dropped off their kids to us yesterday and haven't picked them up."

Now there's a "they." More than one person is missing.

After exhausting the who, what, when, where, how and why, I got this: His niece and her husband dropped off their kids so they could have a weekend trip alone. The couple is out of town but not answering calls and they're a couple of hours late picking up their kids. So, Uncle called, and now we're standing in front of his niece's house.

He doesn't have keys to the house. No lights are on. I

can't force entry even if they wanted me to because all we have here is a late pick up.

After my barrage of questions, I tell him and his tribe gathered behind him, "I can't do anything. All I can do is—" Mid-sentence, a breath exhaled inside my ear. My head involuntarily jerked toward a window on the second story. The interior of the house is black.

In the lowest possible whisper, again in my ear, "We're in here."

Me staring at the house is my non-verbal communication saying, "Nobody fucking talk to me, don't talk to each other in my presence, everybody shut the fuck up."

I'm standing with this family, but the "I" behind my eyes leaves my body and walks to the fence. "I" climb up. Now "I'm" on the overhang. "I" press my face against the window.

I hear it again, "We're in here."

A woman and man lay still, ghost white and dead. Porcelain white because their bodies have drained of blood. The woman's face tells me, "We're in here." Not with her mouth. I hear her voice projected from behind her eyes, landing behind mine.

The uncle interrupts me, "Are you alright?"

I peel my head away from staring at the house.

I'm alright.

They won't be alright.

I tell the uncle, "I'm sorry. All I can do at this moment is write this report and just keep trying to call them." As I drive away, they're still congregating in front of the house, feeling that the police are useless. I lock eyes with the uncle as I drive away. He knows I saw something, but I'm not telling him.

For my sister, these stories are endless. The ones where I hear and see things. They're now met with, "Yeah, yeah,

yeah." It's not so much dismissive as it is unnecessary to narrate constantly. When someone is color blind or deaf in one ear, you don't have to bring up their disability in every conversation.

But, this time, I'm giving direction to Cece.

All she had to do was turn a lock.

I didn't tell her about the missing person's vision, but I am imploring her to take precautions without a lengthy explanation.

I work a 4/10 in patrol. Four days a week, 10 hours a day. Each off day is dedicated to one function. My first day off is to take my mom to Costco and stock her up for what feels like the weekly impending zombie apocalypse. Do we need this much spam, rice and toilet paper?

Mom's television has been on since the early morning. She tunes in to the Filipino Channel, which broadcasts morning church services. She prays along every day. We cycle through the news before we leave. The uncle I spoke to the night before is being interviewed. It turns out, he and the family waited until I left, and then they broke into the house. He broke down in tears as he recalled, "They were dead inside." He gave the news a picture of his niece and her husband on their wedding day. This was the second time I saw his niece's face. In the picture, her beautiful round-cheeked face was alive and fair-skinned, with warm blood flowing beneath the surface. The same face I saw but hollow.

It was a murder-suicide.

She wanted me to find her first before her family, but due to laws of the land I couldn't champion her last earthly request.

I failed.

Again.

Pushing the shopping cart through each Costco aisle, I imagine the woman's last moments. The husband shot and killed her, then turned the gun on himself. The news didn't give out those details, but that's what happened. When it comes to domestic violence, offenders grow up seeing their fathers use violence to resolve conflict. So, to a young man or woman, violence is an option. The husband who pulled the trigger saw no other resolution to whatever issues they were having. Infidelity. Financial issues. I apologized to that woman's soul, but my sentiment faded into the ether because she was no longer here. My opportunity to communicate with her was when she asked me to find her, and I used my job as the reason not to help.

Cece calls me while I'm in the refrigerator section. I wave off the lady wearing a hairnet who is offering me samples of apple strudel. This phone call better mean something.

No "Hello." No "What are you doing?" She goes right into it.

"You were right."

Again. I'm immediately irritated. Right about what? I'm right about almost everything, so I think.

She says, "About my place being broken into."

I go cop mode, "Alright, let's do this my way. Answer all the who, what, when, where, how and whys."

"You don't have to be an asshole." She fires back, derailing this conversation from finding out what happened and now arguing with her in Costco.

"You were right about the other day." She explains her "Okaaaaay" response. She says her boyfriend called her from the street, wanting to visit her and stay the night. Cece told him she had work the following day. To that, he said he's coming to see her anyway. She told him she was gonna lock the door and to that, he answered, "I'm gonna climb in the kitchen window."

"Norm, when you called he was sitting right next to me. I let him in to shut him up. You were on speaker phone and he heard the whole thing. When you hung up he didn't say anything to me and just left."

I push the cart from aisle to aisle, chin down, eyes up.

Cece and her friends are in serious relationships headed to marriage. Her college mates are on fixed career paths based on their chosen majors. After that, career, kids and retirement. She's only a couple of years older than me, and I see my friends on that conveyor belt.

I was supposed to switch places with that little white kid who got kidnapped and killed. Now, I constantly detect that ever present harmful ill intent that some men can't control. And it's incessant. I've always fallen behind in school but progressed in grades because my parents paid tuition. Now, I'm falling behind in adulting. But I have penance to pay, and you don't. Must be fucking nice.

# 8

## GENTLEST GENTLEMAN

### SPRING 1997

In the days that followed Dad's burial, Mom whimpered from the kitchen before the sun came up, the time she'd usually be praying the rosary. I didn't want to go to her and give her an awkward side hug. My sister Cece cried. Seeing my older brother, Michael, cry pissed me off. This family didn't need one more person crying to verify the world was inverted. And Mom needed strong men standing in front of her.

Dad's death wasn't a surprise.

While I was in the police academy, he fell down the stairs. After his two previous open heart surgeries and being confined to his corner chair, the fall sped up his death process. A blood clot formed from one of his legs, and it traveled to his brain, causing a stroke or aneurysm. It's hard to remember. It hurts to look back. Back in the hospital, they hooked him up to a ventilator. His face was frozen in that moment as you're gagging and about to vomit. His skin was gray, and his eyes were so puffy he looked like a frog.

Probably a week before Dad died, and after an academy training day, I raced across the Bay Bridge with my police badge in my pocket. Police Officer Trainees were ordered to leave their badges and guns at the training facility as we hadn't graduated, weren't sworn in and were still civilians. But the badge would indicate to my father that I was able to help my mom financially, and he didn't have to worry about me doing "nothing" with my life. He wasn't worried about Cece or Michael because they were about to have high-powered degrees and corresponding careers. Square pegs. Square holes.

My mom was stuck with medical bills and was about to be alone, so, at the very least, I wouldn't be this thousand-yard staring family liability.

The nursing staff were repositioning Dad and resetting his ventilator. He was about to have emergency surgery to alleviate the pressure in his brain. I positioned myself in his line of sight, reached into my pocket and cupped my badge, waiting for the moment when he saw me.

His head flopped in my direction.

I held out my badge like I busted him, "Look, Dad."

His eyes couldn't focus, but he heard me and knew his head was faced in my direction.

He slurred, "I want to die."

Memories of Dad destroying the heavy bag are faint. My physical strength and boxing skills eclipsed his when I was a teenager, but that doesn't help me make sense that he's not gonna be here much longer. He's supposed to die of old age. His ignorant choice to smoke and eat death row meals not only killed him, it strained all of us.

I gave up the right to cry or feel sorry for myself because I'm alive in place of someone who isn't. People get killed, die of overdoses, commit suicide or abuse their bodies to the point of suffocating themselves. No one goes out gracefully.

Nurses replaced tubes, changed sheets, reset monitors

and moved around me as if I weren't in the room. They handled Dad like an attachment to the ventilator.

I punch down at my own rising grief.

My grandparents from the Philippines lived with us when I was a toddler. When I'd go to their room I'd sit by the space heater. It had exposed horizontal wires that would buzz, glow and smell like burnt dust as it heat the room. My Lola would yell at me to back away. My Lolo knew I wasn't stupid enough to touch the wires and knew I fell into another world staring at the orange glow.

After Dad died I took no time off. I worked, slept and repeated. Mom will not see me cry.

One afternoon, I lay in exhaustion. I dozed off and had another bout of sleep paralysis. This time, flames started burning the bottom of my feet. My mattress caught fire somehow. I have to get up and put it out, but I can't. I can't move. The heat, like that exposed wire from my grandparent's space heater, moved over my shins. This searing heat squeezed sweat out of my pores. Now, this heat was on my thighs. Someone or something was waving a torch over me. I couldn't move my head to see the source of the heat or leap to fight back. Nothing, meaning no thing, was holding me down. Hands weren't pressing down on my shoulders. Then "it" moved over my pelvis, stomach and chest.

There's no way my brain or eyeballs could withstand this heat. They were about to melt in moments, and I was going to die in my sleep. As it reached my head, it felt like pressure right before a balloon pops.

Now, it felt like a single glowing, burning coal leaving through the crown of my skull.

When I lifted my head, the outline of my body was on the bed sheet. It was moist and dark, like someone had pulled me out of the dryer too early. A teaspoon of sweat pooled on top of my sternum. I propped myself up on my elbows.

The urge to cry for my Dad was gone.

I tested myself: I held my father in my mind and heart and but sadness didn't accompany him. That heat scorched grief from my body. I was a rookie cop in Oakland. Grieving a dead parent wasn't helping my focus.

I regret not having a better relationship with Dad. Mom was on birth control with an IUD when she became pregnant with me. Dad got a boy and a girl and I was the oops. I feel Dad's love for me, but I was unexpected, so he delegated parenting to Michael and Cece. By the time I came around, Dad was tired and, knowing what I know now, the best way to show I loved him was to be invisible. You kidding me? That's my factory setting. I wince at the physical pain he endured. He was consumed with his illnesses, and I am certain he wanted the best for me but didn't have anything left for me. I didn't have my siblings' intelligence. He, rightfully, was concerned I was only built for fighting, gangs and, eventually, drugs.

An early memory of Dad was sitting next to him on the floor as he watched boxing. He was drinking a cup of coffee and I knocked it over. I ran for my life like a rat when you turn on the light. I embedded myself in that space between the refrigerator and the wall. Michael and Cece grabbed hold of one of my arms and were cracking up while pleading with me, "He's not mad!" It took the two of them to pull me out. I was still in diapers, so I slipped right out of that crevice.

They dragged me back to Dad like I was an escaped prisoner avoiding execution.

I didn't want to see his face.

The only safe space to hide now was beside him,

breathing slowly, avoiding eye contact and not distracting him from watching boxing.

I still feel him stroking my forehead with his hands which smelled like Lucky Strikes. The only man I've ever feared was the gentlest of all men.

# 9

# THE FACE

## WINTER 1999

You want to be the first cop on the shift to key the mic and announce, "Hold the air!" That instructs everybody to stop, drop and listen for a location. More importantly, it declares, "I'm doing real police work!" Turning a page in the lore of OPD. Where does everyone need to haul ass with their lights and sirens? It's gonna be a car chase or a foot chase with bad guys trying to get away. This is Oakland, after all. Oaktown. Baghdad by the Bay. The Wild West. On top of that, Y2K is around the corner. The global computer crash is imminent, the world is unraveling, and this is all a precursor to the apocalypse. Come get some.

My squad mate, James, broke radio silence with, "3L21, hold the air." My first reaction was, "Fuck. He's gonna get on the board with a felony arrest." I don't want him not to get one, but I have to get one to justify my existence as an Oakland patrol cop.

So far, during my shift all I got was a couple FC's of some dudes at a dope corner. FC's or Field Contacts come in handy when a shooting or murder occurs in that area.

When you fail to make a dope arrest, all you can do is document that contact with a card as proof you're out there in the mix.

Over the radio, James broadcasts, "I'm in pursuit of two possible stolen vehicles."

That's probably true. It's night. Car thieves think that not putting the headlights on will cloak their activity if they steal a car. As you just visualized, it does the opposite. A car flying at high speeds at night with its lights off is like walking into a jewelry store with a hoodie and sunglasses at noon. But saying "possible stolen" on the air is like saying bad guys are throwing dope and guns out the window so the supervisors won't cancel your chase.

James updates that they're about to get on the freeway.

I'm still flooring the gas pedal to get to his location while the radio is tied up with officers wanting to hear themselves telling the world they're coming to help James. While the radio was clogged, he got on the freeway and was, in fact, chasing two cars.

He was able to interrupt the chatter and broadcast, "The lead car is throwing dope and guns." Oh shit. Jackpot.

I'm equidistant to the on-ramp to pick up the dope and guns and from the on-ramp to join in on the chase and catch some bad guys. This feels like coins spilling from a slot machine into a plastic cup. For him.

Go left.

Pick up shit.

Go right.

Get bad guys.

I'm not picking shit up. That's a rookie's job.

James was able to update that the rear car peeled off to an exit, so he chose to stay with the car responsible for the dope and guns. Felonies galore times the quantity of recovered narcotics and guns. I joined the pursuit at the termination point, where the suspect vehicle lost control and crashed a couple of exits ahead. The driver and occupants were defiant when taken out of their car. "You motherfuckers got shit on us." True. Nothing may be in the car now, but the baggies and guns on the freeway will have one of their fingerprints on a "Gat" or baggie of dope.

That's what the Field Training Officer and his rookie were collecting after stopping freeway traffic. As we were cuffing and stuffing the driver and passengers, a patrol unit over the radio yelled, "Officer down!"

The car that James was chasing that exited the freeway found an overpass overlooking where the narcotics and guns were at rest. When the officers stopped traffic, approached the evidence and started to pick it up, one of the occupants from the suspect vehicle on the overpass aimed his rifle at the officers. The suspect shot and killed the rookie officer who was focused on picking up evidence. No vest could stop that rifle round rocketing the distance of two football fields in one second. Rifle bullets traveling at that speed liquify, then disintegrate flesh.

Weeks later, when the suspect was caught, I think he said he was aiming at the overhead patrol lights as a distraction so his friends could get away.

Every available Oakland Police Officer, California Highway Patrol Officer and Alameda County Deputy converged on the scene of the downed officer. I get there but in the opposite direction of the freeway. Both directions of the road were locked up for one whole day after. The rookie is on his back, looking at the sky. Supervisors scream at officers to lock down off- and on-ramps. Officers from all agencies pace in place, rapidly scanning the overpasses and streets parallel to the freeway. Where's the rifleman that's taking aim at me? To those who want to pick off some cops, we are now the fish in the barrel. Police and news helicopters flying overhead make face-to-face communication impossible without yelling.

Also, when the suspect was named and caught I remembered I had FC'd him earlier that day. The intersection of my life timeline and that thing that will end me approaches convergence.

In the middle of all this, the dying rookie stared up at the stars in the East Bay sky, oblivious to the commotion swirling around him. I know that look.

The moment before Dad died, his eyes darted in all directions before he looked at me one last time. An opaque white film covered his eyes, making him look like a blind person. Beside Dad, a voice beyond me came through my mouth with a message for him as he was passing. "You can go. You did your job. You can rest now. I love you. I'll take care of mom." Dad took his last breath and was gone.

This rookie let everything behind him go and was floating home. Leaving behind this perpetual shit show.

I drop my shoulders.

I feel the shooter is in the wind and he's using this congregation of cops as his smoke bomb to ghost himself. This shot cop's spirit has left this body on the freeway.

To honor him, the City of Oakland would name a stretch of freeway after him.

They could have that shit.

Someone yelled at me because I took a moment to lean on the center divide and stare at the rookie's lifeless face. Like Dad's. Like that Asian lady from the missing person turned murder-suicide. And like the countless dead faces I'd see over the next quarter century. I guess I was yelled at because I was doing nothing. I had to write something down, talk on my radio, or look panicked like everybody else.

I don't know if this feeling in my chest was new or if it had been there all along.

I do not want to be a police officer anymore.

I cringe driving to work, putting on my bulletproof vest, uniform and safety belt. My love for the profession never returned. The culture of turning a page to get an arrest, write tickets, or reduce crime is a reward button with diminishing returns. People will never stop trespassing, stealing from and harming each other. The Police believe they can re-stuff Pandora's box by enforcing laws. What does the data show from the beginning of recorded time?

My shift tagged the graveyard shift to stand guard for homicide investigators to map out the murder scene. The graveyard eventually tagged the following day shift in. My body is exhausted. We couldn't leave until we handed in our supplemental reports.

I'm gonna stay at my mom's so she can see that I'm alive. When she turns on the news, she knows I'm downstairs sleeping in Dad's old room.

When I woke up, the television was on with the news showing constant reports of the shooting on the freeway. Mom prayed the rosary non-stop for the fallen officer. The Roman Catholic rosary is a sequence of prayers corresponding to the beads on something that looks like a necklace with the crucifixion of Jesus as the central pendant. Coincidentally, my last name means "of the Rosary" in Spanish.

Mom shakes her head and winces in pain for the fallen's family. I try to ease her concern that I could be the next dead cop by telling her, "Mom, I take every precaution to be safe." She stared at the TV, and every channel she switched to had coverage of the killing. Under her breath, she said dismissively, "Oh, I never worried about you."

For the previous years, her attentional resources have been spent on managing Dad's decline and death and paying for Cece and Michael's college. No one will admit this, but Dad not being here is a relief. He's not suffering, and neither are we. Cece started her Biotech career, and Michael caught his stride in finance.

I mimicked being a student, bringing minimal attention to myself. My report cards were coded with "D's" and some "C's," while Cece and Michael excelled and demonstrated academic excellence. Attention was diverted to their accolades, which I never envied. I didn't want eyes on me, nor did I deserve eyes on me.

The next time you flip a coin to choose between two decisions, pay attention to what you want while the coin is in the air. It wasn't fate that I chose to go right and join the chase. I decided to turn right for testosterone and dopamine. This wasn't a protective premonition to avoid death. I'm pretending to be a cowboy, and the chase was the only real choice instead of evidence retrieval.

Why the fuck do I see the shit I see? I'm not talking about cop shit. It's not to keep me safe. From moment to moment I mitigate my risk by controlling where I stand, what side of the street to walk on, who I make eye contact with, when to cross the street and what volume to speak at with an agitated person. Do I up nod, throw up a peace sign or completely ignore that fool that's a block away?

You won't catch me slippin'. I stay ready so I don't have to get ready.

Something has shifted in me today, and it's not from sleep deprivation. When my eczema flared up as a kid the pain in my face would pulsate. Now, from the crown of my skull to the bottom of my feet, I'm pulsating to the rhythm of my heart. Before, it would take me a moment to look at someone and see a puffy cushion of dim light around their silhouette. Now people look distorted, like they're reflecting heat waves. It's happening now, like right now, in this moment. My ability to see different things isn't subtle. Being a cop poured gas on that fire, and where I previously had to go to an ashram and meditate to shift into another dimension, it is now accessible in this moment.

The facial expressions people wear to cover what's beneath are easily moved out of the way like a handheld masquerade ball mask on a stick. I can't turn "it" off, so I go to bookstores for a book bunker so I don't have to feel people. Everywhere I look, pinwheels of energy swirl and whirl like the top view of a tornado. Closing my eyes makes it worse.

Meditation, prayer, massage, acupuncture, Tai Chi, Yoga, Boxing dial down the noise. I pass Japantown when I drive the grid. It has a spa with a sauna and steam room. The extreme heat distracts, numbs and pauses my monkey mind. It's co-ed day, so couples fawn over each other forehead to forehead. Get a room. The baking heat distracts me enough to take a nap. I abruptly woke up. I must have snorted because couples in their towels contain their giggles. Maybe I farted.

I default to driving the grid to induce highway hypnosis so I could fall asleep.

I'm still staying at Mom's so she can see me alive one last time before I start my work week.

I didn't time this shit right. Out of my bedroom window, the dusk sky fades to black, and then dawn will break. I toss and turn.

A mild earthquake nudges the house like a soft bounce to put a baby to sleep.

It's not an earthquake. It's my bed.

Here we fucking go again.

I break a cold sweat like breaking a fever. It's not the ambient temperature that activated my sweat. My body is priming for another vision.

I cannot catch a fucking break.

I'm gonna hear it.

Anticipate it so it doesn't freak you out.

On cue, the whisper, "Norman."

This isn't in my head.

As I lay on my back, it's coming from the ceiling.

The random splattering of stucco offers the opportunity to see rabbits, horses, dragons. Like clouds shapeshifting.

A slightly imperceptible face that can only be seen by squinting separates from the stucco clouds and animal shapes. This face isn't flat on the ceiling canvas. It's a face punctured through the ceiling like a bank robber using pantyhose as a mask, but, in this case, this shit isn't funny.

I lock eyes with it because I know I'm fatigued, grieving, and my imagination, coupled with my extra vision, makes me see shit that either isn't there or shit that other people can't see. If I stare at it long enough, it'll fade.

Nope.

We're staring at each other. My bed shakes more, and the invisible hands that have contact with my bed grip and crawl closer to my body like a tarantula. The sheets tighten underneath me.

"Row, row, row your boat gently down the stream.

Merrily, Merrily, Merrily, life is but a dream."

I sing.

There it is. I know what's happening. My dream and wake cycles overlap.

I'm so mentally, physically and spiritually spent that I can't discern different states of consciousness.

That face isn't Dad's or Lolo's.

It's transparent, but the texture of the face reflects the moonlight coming into the room. Eyebrows, eyes, nose, mouth hovering at the height of the ceiling. It's staring at me, not blinking. I couldn't read the expression behind the no expression. Slight tension in its brow. Its eyes are wide open. I gather this visual information in that glimpse.

I turn on my side.

Y'know, years of this insomnia shit are gonna tattoo bags under my eyes. Western doctors are gonna tell me stress triggers these hallucinations and then they'll prescribe me meds. Deafen the symptom, keep me on a payment leash, feed the pharma machine.

I turn on my back, eyes toward the ceiling.

THE FACE is nose to nose with me.

It's not leaning over the bed. It's hovering horizontal over me.

I'm fucking awake.

THE FACE wants me to see it. None of this peek around the corner or hang out in my peripheral ninjitsu.

It's still not blinking or swaying from breathing.

It's closer than nose to nose.

We're brow to brow.

Its eyes fixed on mine and locked with the observer behind my eyes and inside my skull.

Your eyes are the closest organ to your brain, or your eyes are an extension of your brain. The brain is the most complex object known to man in the universe. It creates the hologram of the perceived universe.

We hold. THE FACE crossing the doorway of my eyes and observing me from the inside. It's about to talk inside my head bypassing my ears.

THE FACE IS JUST. FUCKING. STARING. AT. ME.

... Hi?

This thing has crossed the membrane from the other world, through my ceiling and is now overlapping my frontal lobe.

The ghosts I've seen communicate through imagery, distort the ambient atmosphere or whisper to get your attention. This entity is solid and wants something from me. Run, Norm.

FUCK. THIS.

I grip the corner of my blanket and turtle shell until the fucking sun comes up.

When I wake, I feel something I've never felt before.

Alone.

---

# 10

# I CAN STILL FEEL THE COLD

## PHILIPPINES 1950

The University of the Philippines School of Nursing is a couple miles south of Manila. It's the 1950s, and Mom was the first in her *barrio* to leave for college. The first to leave for anything, really. If you're picking up on the Spanish influence, your ears are attuned. An aside. The Spanish occupied the Philippines from 1565 to 1898 and did the same in Mexico from 1521 to 1820. As your intellect suspects, pollination occurs.

Back to sweltering Manila, where the heat waves distort the horizon wherever you turn your head. Mom is doing her clinicals in Labor and Delivery — what would be her focus for the following four decades.

A pregnant patient immediately recognized Mom and was put at ease. The woman, accompanied by the soon-to-be father, had never stepped in an air-conditioned building with tiled floors before. Mom's presence was a prayer answered and a divine guide in this sterile and cold environment.

When the woman went into labor, Mom reflected while looking out the window, "I felt something was wrong. Like the baby was slipping away." Mom instinctually gave the woman ice water. Once that cold hits the womb, it'll awaken a fading fetus. But it didn't help.

The baby was stillborn. The first of many in her career. But the first. Procedurally, stillborns are stored in the frigid morgue in the basement. There's no way this couple had the means to pay for both an autopsy and authorized dead baby transport several hours south of Manila. The body of the baby remained as the property of the province.

The childless woman and man were sent back on a bumpy and dusty trek to their hometown on one of those obnoxiously ornamented "Jeepneys." I wonder what that moment was like when they arrived back home and how long it took for the village to realize the loss. Or, in reverse, how the couple pulling up saw beaming faces, knowing in moments that wouldn't be the case.

Mom is now 92, and this is my first time hearing this story. She can't hear nowadays. But her mind is intact. She knows how much my eczema ointment cost in 1976 and whose birthday is this month and the next. Point to a date on the calendar, and if it has significance to our family, she'll recall it. She has savant memory and *Bruja* instincts. Look that up. I'm not cursing myself.

I remember one time when Michael and his homies were hanging out in front of the house. Dré tripped backward over the boombox blasting Run DMC, hit his head on the curb and had a seizure. Mom flew downstairs, lay Dré on his side and used a spoon to fish out and hold his tongue in place so he didn't choke on it. I can still hear Dré waking up from his seizure, squealing in pain and my mom stroking his head, "It's okay, Anák. You're going to be okay."

Over my life, I've made at least a hundred Philippine care packages, or Balikbayan boxes, filled with pens, notebooks, socks, activity books, medicine, handwritten letters and anything her hometown could use. Mailing cash in envelopes sealed in bigger envelopes evolved into wiring money to her living brothers and sisters, nieces, nephews, Godchildren or anyone with their hand out. You give what you can.

When I went to the Philippines with her after Dad died, I witnessed random people stopping, grabbing her hand and requesting, "Máno, po." As nameless people placed my mom's hand to their forehead, they not only closed their eyes, but shut them in prayer.

You picked up on it, again. People requested Mom's hand, or máno, for her to bless them. In this dimension of the planet, Elders are designated reps of God's love, care and wisdom Mom is revered.

Back at the hospital over 70 years ago and moved by her heart, Mom ignored the chain of command, stood tall in front of the superintendent and Jedi mind tricked him, "What if the document indicated the baby was born and released to the family?" Technically, the baby exited the mother and was *born*. She projected to the Super, sign the release paper and turn your head for the *"released to the family"* part. He sifted through piles of paper, signed and approved with a nod without making eye contact.

Self-assigned, Mom carried this stillborn wrapped inside an ice pack and boarded a Jeepney. The unbuckled passengers sitting on splintered wooden planks shoulder bumped each other for hours, jostling over unpaved country roads.

"I stared out the window the whole time. No one asked me what I had."

Mom is completing a sticker puzzle while telling this story. She's using tweezers to peel the stickers and place them in their designated spots — kinda like paint by numbers.

"It was like a celebration when I got off the Jeepney. Some cried, but they were just happy they can give the baby a proper burial. You know, Norman, I come from an uneducated fishing town. These people would have accepted not ever seeing their baby. Child mortality is expected. I could not let that happen."

She put the tweezers down and looked out the window and into the infinite distance. Mom rubbed her thighs with her 92-year-old wrinkled hands. A single tear ran down her cheek.

"I can still feel the cold."

## 11

## WHAT'S IN TEXAS?

### SUMMER 1999

Before my graveyard shift, I would back myself up in the corner of my cafe in San Francisco's North Beach district. Think little Italy. Philosophers and poets like Krishnamurti, Bukowski and Diogenes, who see the bullshit of organized society, win my heart and attention. There's a comfort in reading their thoughts, exposing middle-of-the-road living. We all smelled the American Dream sales pitch, and here we are, punching clocks en masse. We were sold and bought the idea that spending life hours at employment equates to car payments, rent, grocery bills and a shared struggle. I'm making that trade just like you, but reading about the absurdity makes me a millimeter more aware. I know I'm in a play and it sucks.

I still covered my paperbacks with a homemade book cover made out of a brown paper grocery bag. A carryover habit from grade school. It prevents people from striking up conversations with me. To this day, only one person has asked me what I'm reading.

A row of silver-haired men and women with bad breath line the entrance of this cafe. Even without a newspaper in hand, their postures remain hunched over, and their faces still pissed at whatever they just read. They are the remaining witnesses to the San Francisco Hippie counterculture of the "Turn on, Tune in and Drop out" generation of the 1960s. I'd catch their synchronized eye rolls as cleancut Yuppies would trespass on this old San Francisco haunt. Yuppies traveled in packs, in business attire minus the tie, just getting off their shifts in the financial district. Yuppie culture overlapped with the dot-com boom, so the young and wealthy felt immortal walking around like they owned the joint. Put them on a bus and drop them off in the projects, and they wouldn't make it out without being robbed, shanked or tuned up.

What made me want to punch them in the mouth was their volume. My conversation between you and me is just that. For them, you are an audience member, and you're welcome. It's important to them, so by default, it's important to you, and you'd benefit from them talking about golf plans this weekend. Nope. Bop! Right in the mouth.

Weekly, this refined, bespoke dressed, porcelain white-skinned Americanized Korean woman would bring her daughter in to get a cup of coffee to go. Light-skinned Asians are classy and intellectual, genetically predisposed for upper management positions and job posters. Filipinos are like jungle Asians. Field workers, knife wielding, unsophisticated and very brown. This woman would walk in with her nose turned up even before she saw me. Asian genetic colorism default to look down on me. The length of the line would determine her patience with her impatient daughter. The line was long on this day, and she huffed out loud, which I didn't care for. She must have felt my disapproval of her indecent public display of irritation because she locked eyes with me from across the cafe. Me, this brown-skinned, shaved head dude hiding behind a book was mad dogging her. Awkward, Norm. I cut eye ties and focused back on reading how Diogenes told Alexander the Great to get the fuck out of his way because he was blocking the sun. Gangster shit.

I never had to pay for a mocha as long as I let the barista, my longtime friend Zeke, sit thigh-to-thigh with me on his breaks. Now and then, he'd offer, "You want a blowjob?" With a pleasant smile and soft eyes, I'd respectfully respond, "I'm good, Zeke." The way I said it was like I just got one, which I never did. I couldn't say the sentence, "I don't want my dick sucked by a man" because I loved Zeke like a brother. The discomfort I felt was incestuous. I'd join him on smoke breaks, talk about who he's dating and how much debt he's in, and I'd tell him about cop shit.

One time on a break, he took a drag and exhaled, "Have you ever fucked a man?"

"No."

I think I answered so fast it must have sounded like, "Fuck, no."

I wanted to adjust mid-convo with "Not yet" out of respect for him and because it would create room that I didn't harbor any ickiness about his sexuality. "Not yet" would have added endless quantum branches to this topic.

He looked at me from the corner of his eye and said, "You should try it."

I softened my face and nodded, "I've never been in that situation."

I felt this conversation was just beginning and that his strategy was attrition. Like, the longer we talked about gay sex I'd just say, "Fuck it. Let's have sex, Zeke." This is what women must think of when dealing with obvious and aggressive men. Like that's men's strategy. Like, "If I talk long enough about it, she'll realize that she wants to do the horizontal mambo with me." It was at that moment I decided I'd never ask, hint, Jedi mind trick or breadcrumb a woman to sleep with me. If that meant I'd be a monk for the remainder of my timeline, then so be it. Seeing creepiness is just ... blech. And Zeke wasn't even pushing the issue.

In between taking his next drag he added, "I thought you were gay."

"Really?" I was one part curious about what energy I was emitting, and one part flattered.

I'm Metrosexual. I know that much. Since I earned money I got facials, massages, went to the chiropractor, bought cologne from Macy's, got acupuncture, reiki and the yoga, tai chi and boxing never stopped. I took a year of ballet because I heard the legendary San Francisco 49er wide receiver Jerry Rice did it to improve his athletic prowess. So, I got the look and posture, whatever that means.

Gay dudes in San Francisco are put together. It's not that I took a page from their book as much as I'm trying to frame and preserve myself at this age. I just wrote a lie. I do all those non-western modalities because I still want superpowers.

Zeke gave me the up down, "You're always by yourself. I've never seen you with a woman."

Yeah. What girl would want to stand beside a short dude with braces and discolored and inflamed eyelids? I ran my thumb on my eyelid out of habit to feel for the flakiness that hadn't been there for years. I aged out of my eczema but I forgot. As time progresses, I still bring that frightened boy along for this ride.

I prolonged this conversation with, "Have you ever been with a woman?"

I immediately regretted going into overtime.

He had that story on deck and went right into, "I was dating this guy who was dating a woman. The woman said she wanted to see her boyfriend fuck a man." Enter Zeke. "We started doing it and she joined in. When I tried to put my dick in her I went limp."

In my head, "Zeke! That's it. That's me when I visualize ... Strike that. I've never visualized putting my dick inside a man but imagining that deflates my hypothetical and future boners."

He doesn't know I'm having this conversation with him. He just sees me nodding. To him, I'm moisturizing my mind for gay sex.

I kiss Zeke goodbye as I'm off to drive the grid.

You'd think I'd sleep better since I'm not interrupted by visions and whispers. Ever since I turned from THE FACE, I see only what's in front of me. As it is. Nothing more. No swirls, whirls or vibrations.

In boxing, martial arts and warfare tactics, distance equals reaction time. Trying to understand THE FACE, I had both time and distance to process that night. Demons don't kill humans. They use humans to kill humans. They influence. THE FACE had a stern look of admonishment. But, what the fuck was I doing wrong in life? I didn't have the balls to toe the line and listen like a good boy. I declined the message and navigated life on routine, hoping that meaning would surface passively. THE FACE had information for me. Or, it was a demon recruiting me. Maybe I'll get it reading or getting signs in increments, but I remember turning away, deafening my ability to see otherness. There are gradations to intelligence. We observe the forms of life below us and study their place in our ecosystem as we all coexist in this habitat. We are not the highest form of intelligence as we look down with the tops of our heads hitting an imaginary capped ceiling. THE FACE wasn't gonna tell me I was gonna die. It had to dumb itself down, lower its vibration and actually lower itself to contact me. What an opportunity I declined to communicate with an above being. Any message could have been a directive to sift through the noise to get to the signal. The signal on how to live with purpose. Who doesn't want that answer in one sentence? Apparently, me.

I made it to the sauna and steam room in Japantown. It's all dudes today. I'm in the steam room when I realize all dudes is code for gay men's day. It rotates. Co-ed, women then men. In the steam room, sound amplifies and reverberates against the wet tiles. I hear dudes chomping each other's mouths. They're straight smacking and suctioning. I become insta-mindful of my own space and look down at one square tile. That's my tile and no one else's. I'm not gonna leave just because I'm surrounded by gay dudes. That's rude and homophobic.

Across from me, a lonely guy with a towel around his waist lounges on his side. He's staring at me. I close my eyes, focus on my breathing and let the clock run on my sweating time. The eucalyptus infused with the steam helps reduce my asthmatic wheezing. When I opened my eyes, the guy across from me was now shoulder-to-shoulder with me. He longingly stares at me, and then his eyes trace my shoulders and zig zag towards my groin. He's stretching his dick like a balloonist would stretch a deflated balloon at a children's party before creating a poodle. He chokes the head of his penis with the reverse "okay" hand symbol. What. The. Fuck. Dude.

At this point, we look like two passengers side by side on a bus taking turns at high speeds. He's leaning into me and I'm leaning away because he wants to kiss me. Why the fuck can't women be this aggressive with me? I'd be like, "Oh, stop it, keep going some more, please!" How do I make that happen, man? I want that.

In my man voice I tell him, "I'm good, man." Not with the softness and open-ended possibility I expressed to Zeke. It's like when you're walking through the mall and the pushy salesperson is about to spray you with perfume. With a stern sense of your boundaries, lift your hand and project, "No, thank you." That energy.

Naked masturbating guy disappeared into the mist and I escaped to my car. I drove home in wet clothes, checking my mirrors. I drove in an erratic pattern and circled blocks, losing my imaginary tail like I was a wanted fugitive or a spy trying to drop a surveillance crew.

I never get rejected by girls because I never approach girls. I knew I wanted to have sex. My anti-insomnia night time checklist included, but was not limited to, hitting the heavy bag until exhaustion, driving the grid to lull myself to sleep and playing either "The Matrix" or "Heat." Lastly, putting in one of my VHS porn tapes was the final effort to reach unconsciousness. A couple closet perverts at work would exchange tapes with me when we got bored with our stash.

Don't leave the tape with "Empire Strikes Back" written on the cover with an asterisk lying around. It's NOT "Empire Strikes Back."

I'd put a bath towel stuffed underneath my bedroom door. Light coming from my room at 4 a.m. means I'm masturbating to pornography. I also put a bath towel on top of my VCR to muffle the rewinding and fast-forwarding. I fast forward through group sex. I had to visualize one on one action. With another guy, I'd be wondering if she got more pleasure from him because his dick was bigger or if he was good looking. Plus, just incidental contact with another dude would break my circuit. And you can forget making eye contact with another naked man.

Victor and I joked that if we were ever in that situation, we'd agree to keep our eyes closed and socks on. That qualifies us as not being completely naked.

Out of the hundreds of scenes I'd pleasure myself to, I was mesmerized by the few women whose faces would display genuine ecstasy. I want to share that with a woman. Just me and her. Most of porn is hitting positions for the camera. Based on Tantra and books on sexuality in the hidden section in the bookstore, I could tell hips would be tilted for show. Some actresses didn't kiss on the mouth, but they'd give blowjobs. After extended research, what turned me on the most were those who lost themselves in each other. It wasn't acting.

Weeks and months flipped off the calendar as I hit cafes before work, punched the clock and stayed awake after my shift.

I went to the cafe to stop obsessing about dying at work. Seeing the faces of those with benign nine-to-fives made me wish I had a paper degree to work in a sterile place. Throughout grade school and high school, I'd be the one with my head turned out towards the window. School is a blur because I didn't pay attention. Now, I wish I had a piece of paper in a frame that would get me safer jobs.

During my work week, without fail, some drunk man would beat his wife, someone would get sexually assaulted, one D-boy will shoot and kill another D-boy over dope. My time as a cop won't put a dent in crime. It won't slow it down. This occurred before me and will continue after I retire. These behaviors are core components to humans. It's part of the hard drive. I heard criminal behavior explained best through Pedophilia. The penal code is written as illegal, and a punishment is assigned. Just because those words are in print doesn't take away some sweaty pervert's desire to fondle an underage kid's genitals. It might sound like a statement of the obvious, but no one should let their guard down because laws and cops exist.

I see that Korean lady. Great tailored outfit as usual. Not off the rack for her. I don't see her kid in tow. She's in line, and I'm in my corner. She looks in my direction, but I'm not looking at her. I see her blurred silhouette above the top of my book. I move my eyes left to right to smokescreen that I'm reading. If she was a dude, she'd be a yuppie.

Oh shit. She's walking toward me. She totally smushed her tits in her shirt. If she sneezed I'd see her nipples.

"What'cha reading?"

Like a dumbass, I look at my own covered book. I might as well have said, "Bitch, if I wanted you to know I wouldn't have covered it." But, that's not why I checked the cover. If it showed the Bhagavad Gita or Khalil Gibran's "The Prophet" I would've asked her what she knew about it so that could be the premise of our conversation. Seemed like a good strategy for convo.

Her perfume dissolves in the back of my throat and I gulp. She has a coating of foundation on her face and a shade of makeup mixed in. There's a book on painting, Alla Prima. Wet on wet it loosely translates to. That's how she applied her make up.

"Oh that's interesting. Are you a philosophy student?"

I must have given my synopsis while I was studying her face.

"I'm actually a cop. I come here to decompress before work."

How do you decompress before an event? You decompress after something. A comes first, then B. It's not B then A. So stupid, Norm. I speak and hit the ball back to her. "I've seen you in transit with your kid." In transit? Is she a fucking passenger bus?

She doesn't notice my mini-stroke in the conversation part of my brain and goes right into, "I have a break, finally. My daughter is with 'the father' for the weekend." She slumps, allowing herself to enjoy her coffee. Then, with her eyes, she traces my shoulders. Did a bird shit on me before I came in?

"Skinny Norm" is another nickname at work. My clothes hang off me and I might look emaciated from the neck up. Great. She thinks I'm shaped like a toothpick. It would be odd to take off my shirt and show her I walk around at six percent body fat and that years of yoga and boxing have chiseled my frame.

Ask her what she does for work. It's polite.

"What business are you in?"

That wasn't bad, Norm.

Delight flashes across her face. This is a good conversation.

"I'm all over the place, meaning ALL over the place. I'm a regional manager for a hotel chain from Texas all the way to the west coast."

Comment on that to keep the conversation going. You've seen people do that.

"That's gotta be fun and challenging."

She comes right back, "It should be, but the father drops the ball with our kid."

She's divorced. I'm a fart smeller. I mean a smart fella. I'm occupied with getting through one work week while she's balancing a career and raising a kid. The number one cause of divorce is marriage. Noted.

"What about you? What's it like being a cop?"

I cave in, remembering I have to take off for work in a few minutes. I dread knowing I'll find a dead body this week or I'll be "motherfucked" for being a racist. I give the obligatory, "Man, it's crazy."

She leans toward me and I make sure my eyes stay on her eyes. That's equally as uncomfortable as getting caught looking at her chest. Front sight focus, Norm. In firearms marksmanship, you're taught to focus on the front sight of the gun. Your target should be blurred. Doesn't make sense, but it ensures alignment.

I flossed, scraped my tongue, brushed my teeth and gargled with apple cider vinegar then a splash of hydrogen peroxide before I left the house, so I'm nearly positive my breath doesn't stink.

This is the most relaxed I've seen her. Coming from or going to work and towing her kid around makes her fidgety and rude to service staff. I don't like her, but I can't be rude.

"What's the craziest thing you've seen?"

Why is she asking about my work?

There's a softness contrary to her always being in a rush. I don't like feeling I got a timer on my responses so I throw out a vague and easily digestible soundbite. "It's called Baghdad by the Bay for a reason."

She giggles a little too hard at that dry ass statement.

I check my watch.

She inches back to her original position, "You gotta go now? I'll let you go."

I heard someone say, "Nice chatting with you" the other day, and it sounded like a nice button on a conversation. I had that phrase on deck ready to launch.

I tried it out, "Nice chatting with you."

Weird. She didn't say anything back. She's just looking at

me like when I size up a guy I might have to fight. She's biting her lip. Huh?

As I put my covered book and notebook into my backpack, she lowers her voice and pushes close to the side of my face. "Hey, maybe you could fly out to Texas and meet me there. I'm out there for up to a week sometimes. You wouldn't have to pay for a room because ... I know the boss." She winks.

I swing my backpack on and ask, "What's in Texas?"

# 12

## CRY FOR ME

### SPRING 2000

Driving the grid expanded to traveling across the Golden Gate Bridge, which is really brick red in color, and getting lost on sidewinding roads. I ended up atop Mount Tamalpais with God's view of the entire Bay Area or surrounded by Redwoods. I'd pull off random exits and find small towns where I was the only brown person in sight. I was about to enter a convenience store that looked like it was restored from the gold mining days when someone's unattended dog started to growl at me. Racist dog.

"It senses your fear." Luna interrupted.

Luna likes me but doesn't like cops. To her, I'm "Little Buddha," and as long as we talk about energy, vibrations, love, service, and God, we're golden.

"Do you have your gun on you?"

I do. But what has that got to do with anything?

"He," the dog, "senses that."

From that point on, I put my gun in the trunk or didn't carry it at all.

Instilling that practice around her probably saved a couple of lives.

On a day off, Luna and I finished a swanky dinner on Van Ness Boulevard in San Francisco. While walking to my car she looked like she was about to cry as she wiped her hand on her pants. Did a bird poop on her hand? Did she bang it on a parking meter?

I check in. "What happened?"

She tried to brush me off. "I'm fine."

I fucking hate that word. I stop in my tracks. She's hurt and hiding it from me.

I order her to respond, "No. What happened?"

Some homeless guy spat on her as we walked past him. This isn't a trial where I get into his psychology with, "Why would you do that?!" "What's wrong with you?!" We know why he did that. She was in his path, and he doesn't give a fuck. There. That's the impetus. Asking or getting into a dialogue with him is delaying. We're all afraid. The fork in the road is to keep moving or provide him with a significant emotional event to adjust his behavior in this present moment. He's done this shit before and you know that. Let's spring this fucking trap.

I B-line it to him, "Apologize."

When he stands up, my forehead lines up with his clavicle.

Great.

He screams, "I didn't spit on your bitch!"

Maybe we should've just walked on...

Nah.

She's not a bitch. She's my friend and I'm going to fuck you up.

I got one shot to knock him out or this scenario is gonna branch out to him stabbing or pummeling me.

He steps closer and leans down, punctuating each word with a head butt.

"I!"

He's not close enough.

"Didn't!"

His bad breath is mixed with alcohol.

"Spit!"

Not yet, Norm.

"On!"

"Your!"

My left foot is forward. I'm in orthodox stance. My left leg is slightly bent and spring-loaded. He thrusts his forehead toward mine when he yells, "Bit-!"

Before "-ch" I launch a left uppercut. It's like he's standing over a metal manhole cover on the street and there's an underground explosion. That piece of metal will be hurling upward toward his jaw. But it's my left uppercut. My favorite punch. When it lands, his head will face the sky and he'll be unconscious.

But at this moment, from his point of view, he's yelling into a short Filipino guy's slanty eyes. He has no idea I'm gonna send his ass into an alternate universe. Right-hand hospital. Left-uppercut cemetery.

I miss. I graze his chin with my knuckles. Instead, I catch a tooth on the way up with my pinky and ring finger knuckle before I fracture his nose. I break my hand in the process.

He steps back and cups his nose. He's wounded but not dead. As he stumbles back, I have one play. Knock him out, or I'm going toe to toe with this NBA-sized homeless man with nothing to lose. My left is broken, but I'm willing to sledgehammer it into his face one more time if it means he'll be unconscious. After each haymaker aimed for the fences, I ducked and slipped, anticipating a counter punch. No punches whizz by my face. He's not throwing back. He has no skill, and I get to tee off on him, but he's so damn lanky. One step backward, and his head is two arm lengths away from me.

He turns, trots away from me, then mumbles through his fingers, covering his mouth, "I'm calling the cops!" Globs of blood drip down his chin, leaving a blood trail away from us.

Violence has its place.

Luna avoided mentioning that people stole, raped and just flat-out attacked people for dominance. This homeless guy highlighted human behavior she intentionally ignores. On the one hand, I do join her in disdain for sick bro cop jock culture. She assumes it exists. I see it in real time. It's mob mentality.

Hurt people do hurt people and I get that people are desperate and make mistakes. On the other hand, accountability is a law. Not a penal code. The law of the jungle. There are consequences to choices. You spit on a woman, you get your ass whooped.

I remember Mom came home from her night shift and was opening up the garage when she was robbed. I heard the aftermath from my bedroom. She yelled for my Dad, doors flew open. Cops came. From my bedroom, I could see strobing red and blue lights reflected off the hill in my backyard. That robber should be held accountable for this: He frightened and hurt my Mom. Taking away that man's freedom doesn't satisfy me. I want to be alone with him. He doesn't deserve death, but nothing says I can't make him feel like he's gonna die.

Luna defended the offenders. "They grew up in poverty and strife." In my head, she took a lamp and moved it from accountability to the circumstances and environment that created the criminal.

Increasing volume and interrupting each other never happened between us and that's what I loved about her regal femininity. I never pushed my sense of right because I felt there was something I was blind to. I knew when to shut up. As in the bookstore, there is new knowledge around the corner. We held space for each other but, like a car with its alignment pulling to one side, we both defaulted to our beliefs of right and wrong and justice and right living as in the tenet expressed by the Buddha.

I wish we never spoke about work because we'd still be together. Maybe.

Our bliss started when I began eating at a restaurant in North Beach where she waitressed. I'd see Yuppies on their lunch break sitting at the counter to be close to her. After they ordered, they'd look at her head to toe and back up again. Luna had a wild mane tamed by either a headband, hair clips or braided into pigtails. My favorite. She had iridescent green eyes that I had to avoid because once I locked in staring I wouldn't break away. Her hair hid her sinewy neck and pronounced clavicle, which was the first indication that she was Olympian level fit. The striations in her neck and shoulders elongated and contracted when she turned her head. For me, to see that under her fair skin meant that it was a combination of genetics or hard work to maintain that level of muscle definition and low body fat percentage. She had to wear a sports compression-type bra to encase her breasts. Despite having a low body fat percentage, she held onto her natural breast size. That suppleness contrasted with her flat stomach with indentations creating shadows to highlight her sectioned abdominal muscles. She was hard inside like me, but as she explained later, "You can get to peak fitness from different roads. Like Yoga and Pilates." She has been a trained dancer since she was a kid. She glided across the floor as if she was traversing a stage. When she greeted me at the door, my bushy eyebrows lined up with her nose. And she was in flats. Her long fingers covered most of the surface area of the menu she would hand me. I understand why every single man stole a glimpse of her unusual and unique beauty.

It didn't take many visits for her to figure out I liked being in the corner facing out. It's not a cop thing. It's a growing up in the Hood thing. I stopped covering my books because I noticed it brought more unwelcome glances. She felt comfortable enough to invade my space while I was reading. I unconsciously blurted, "There's that quote that says lovers don't gaze at each other, but in the same direction." As I took my foot out my mouth, I apologized. "I'm just into this stuff, man." I called her man to snap out of being a creep. It felt like an okay thing to share.

She introduced me to Rumi and we both loved Kahlil Gibran. I kept our interactions to four hits over the net.

Hello.

Hi.

What's new?

Nothing but a whole lot.

Yuppies leaning over the counter, prolonging the appropriate time to converse sickened me and bordered on trespassing.

On a previous failed "meet up," "date," "hangout," whatever you want to call it, I had to learn the hard way to not talk incessantly. From that disastrous interaction, I learned that people occupy the same space and just talk at each other. It's not a balanced listening session. Instead, see for yourself, it's two wind-up toys in a box. This other girl I had a crush on was fixated on speaking about her "friend" that drives fast, doesn't open the door for her and pays more attention to his frat boy friends. So, yes, I was on a date with someone who was talking about their boyfriend. During a lull in the conversation, I brought up Krishnamurti and how he changed my mental paradigm when observing authority figures or organized religion because that felt like a good idea at the time. She returned to complaining mode and it was clear this was going nowhere. The chocolate ice cream in my mouth became my focal point as her voice faded in the background. This ice cream wasn't from a chain. I looked back in the parlor and thought, "They must have a machine where they make this shit on the premises!" I turned her sound off while I was making out with this dense, creamy chocolate in this sugar cone.

When I made it home, I cringed at myself. I was like a 4-year-old child approaching a stranger and talking about his favorite toy. It's important to him, but the child has no clue about social situations. That's me. Still, I'm learning. Still awkward.

I could only shake my head at myself and debrief that disaster as I brushed my teeth before bed.

That's when I saw my mouth.

Real chocolate solidified then dried over my chin, mouth and even the bottom of my nose. That chocolate had cycled through the mummification process and now returned to its solid state on my face. Dehydrated and flaky. How long has that shit been there? There was a point where she fell silent at the ice cream parlor.

When I feel I'm talking too much I tell myself, "Chocolate."

I kept my sentences short with Luna unless she elicited more from me. After a couple visits she figured out the order I never deviated from was Fettuccine Alfredo with chicken strips and a root beer. Even when there were no customers I still kept it to a few pleasantries back and forth. Short interactions prevented girls from looking at my face. My face that didn't have eczema anymore. The remnant habit of pivoting away remained. When I found out she did Yoga AND Pilates and read about religion, I couldn't ask enough about how she saw the world. My aloneness came from not having words to explain how the world looked different to me. Speaking the same language doesn't guarantee connection.

Luna and I were building a bridge toward each other. I'd ask, "Where does your mind go when you dance?" "What's the difference inside you during Yoga and during Pilates?" I never shared my out-of-body experiences with and without Yoga because I was immersed in her responses. She smoked weed, so I investigated, "What's the common state between meditation and being high?" After a conversation, I'd feel so relieved from not talking about myself. I forgot myself, like being in that NOWHERE space.

Giving her my attention contributed to my penance for being alive in place of someone who isn't. When she lit up, finding things about me, I caught myself. Can I enjoy being seen? Sometimes, when it was busy at her restaurant, I'd leave without saying goodbye. It's respect for her work. Who am I to make her pause and acknowledge me in front of other people? But that wasn't her perspective when I came back. "You just disappeared. I thought something happened to you." I explained my rationale. "Oh Buddha, you're cute."

I know I'm not fat Buddha. Hopefully, not gaunt Buddha. She looked out the window to see if any customers were coming in before she turned back to me. I allowed myself to savor her emerald green eyes. Just as the room started to tilt she smiles, leans and asks, "Do you want to go camp-"

"YESSSSS."

Confirm that.

Yes, Luna. Yes. Yes. Yes, I want to be alone with you.

I now know what's in Texas.

I ran my "What's in Texas" story in front of a council of OG vets at the Oakland Police Department and one of them stopped me mid story. "You are the fucking dumbest smart person I know." Apparently, I missed signs that she was interested in me. But, again, cut me some slack, I just started talking and I'm learning to pick up signs like girls asking you to be alone with them. The council closed out, "That's an FBI clue, dumbass."

Luna didn't care we looked like the capital "I" and lower case "i" standing next to each other. When suits asked for her number, I'd seen the smile mask she would use to cover her real face. She didn't look twice at suave fools who would fuel up before hitting up the dance clubs. They'd sweet talk her. Again, at her work. I caught the spectrum of men who tried to court her and then there was me. My day off uniform was a thrift store flannel (I upgraded from the Army Surplus flannel), pressed blue jeans but, still, Doc Marten boots from the Army Surplus Store. Luna looked at me and saw me. Those chumps were just in her field of vision.

She knew about my insomnia and loved to accompany me on grid driving. There was more silence than conversation and when she held my hand I got sleepy. And now we're on our way to go camping. Filipinos don't camp, so I followed her lead. The further I drove away from San Francisco and Oakland the more I'd sink in my seat.

It was mid-week and the campground was empty. I

watched her set up the tent while I held strings and posts in place. She did the real work.

She laughed when I thought out loud, "How useless am I?" After the tent was set she said she was going to take a moment for herself. She disappeared in a tree line. They have bathrooms at the entrance to the site. Taking a shit in the woods is straight hippie when bathrooms are a short walk away. I'm standing downwind and catch a whiff of weed. Ah. She reappears popping a mint in her mouth. I acknowledge her respect with, "You didn't have to go through all that." She wraps her arms around me and puts her forehead to my forehead.

Weed funk is caked in her shirt and hair.

She whispers in my ear, "You're my Buddha."

I'm hard and I tilt my hips back a little like we're at a middle school dance.

It's dark below these trees, but the sky is a blend of blood orange with lavender seeping in. The temperature dropped so fast I saw my breath, so it was time to make it into the tent, which was exactly the same temperature outside. We burrowed into one sleeping bag.

I exaggerate teeth chattering and we giggle. A hint of heat holds between us. Even in faint starlight, I can see her green eyes. We touch our lips, eyes open, staring at each other. We aren't kissing. Behind her eyes, she tells me, "I love you."

I run my fingers through the back of her head. My hand gets jammed with all that hair. I make a fist. I allow myself to look at her. Goddamn, she's pretty. The first girl to tell me she loves me. She's glowing. Her jawline, cheeks and nose are statuesque. This creature invited me to be alone with her. I angle her head, bringing her forehead to my lips so I can kiss it. I lift her head so I can kiss her cheek. Another turn to expose her neck. I kiss there. She's limp and wants me to position her.

We stare.

She pushes me onto my back.

She kisses my neck. Unbuttons my shirt. She resumes kissing my sternum. Stomach. Below my belly button. We help each other unbuckle and take off my pants.

Here.

We.

Go.

A pressure. A touch. What is that?! The tip of one of her fingers is touching the head of my thingy. Okaaaay. Go with it. I've been hard since we crossed the Golden Gate Bridge so this won't make a difference. Dude. Another touch right at the base of my doohickey. I don't look down. I don't need to.

Her hand is in the Hawaiian "Hang Loose" gesture!

What.

The.

Fuck?

She's measuring my dick.

For what?!

Just then, I became the recipient of the Y2K commemorative blowjob. To last, I employed years of breath training by slowing my exhales and lowering my heartbeat. I sank more into the earth, separated by thin tent plastic and an opened sleeping bag. Parts of my spine audibly click, releasing tension as my whole body stopped resisting.

Luna's pleasuring me and I'm hoping she continues.

The porn scenes I consumed lasted an average of 10 minutes. Each sequence is scripted and predictable. Foreplay. Oral sex. Penetration, then climax. I conditioned myself to that 10-minute window to put myself to sleep.

What's happening tonight would follow that sequence but from dusk till dawn.

I turned her onto her back. Like her sequence, I kissed her chest, stomach and below her belly button. I opened my mouth, slack-jawed and lowered my face gently on her yoni.

She retracted, "My God!" aghast like something crept into the tent.

I wasn't slow enough with my lips. In my head I was gentle. I turned her off.

"Your legs!"

Something crawled on me? I slapped away at nothing.

She sat up and squeezed my thighs and calves, "Your legs are ripped!" Her grip wasn't firm enough to squeeze deeper than my skin. Days, weeks, months and years of pushing myself past the pain threshold and into the realm of sadism hardened me. She traced my back and arms and cupped my face with her hands, "As you were."

I flipped through the pages of hand-drawn images of the vagina in my mind. Hours absorbing the anatomy and nomenclature of each fold and region were my mouth's map. When pornstars went down on women they'd lick fast and poke hard, ignoring the woman wincing and pulling away. Luna pressed her body into my lips and tongue and, every now and then, would release a guttural "Uuuhhhhh."

Luna was gone in space, man. We had naturally flowed toward each other as friends. Maybe she saw me as different, not one to approach her with a sales pitch. Whatever I did, she submitted to me. With her legs spread, she's giving me her private and protected essence. And we're enjoying it together. My life force and mental energy interacts with the world through my face and now she's holding my head and face inside the gateway to her womb.

She arched her back, and her whole body stiffened

between the ebb and flow of pressure I'd give with my tongue or puckered lips. At the end of what felt like her body trembling, I kissed below her belly button, on top of her bladder. I kissed my way up to her breasts. Her breasts. The part that I've seen all the men stare at. And tonight, all of her belongs to me.

I whispered in her ear, "I'm not done yet."

I went back down and introduced the tip of my finger into play. From a distance, her moans and occasional screams sounded like she was getting attacked. In this tent, it sounded like a deep weeping and a grieving cry. She was releasing something, and I am her appointed and trusted guardian. I am her protector and her only job is to let go. And she let go. And she melted into the corpse pose and her only sign of life was her chest heaving for air.

She was humming herself back to consciousness. The closer she got back to earth, she started to shake her head side to side. Tears streamed from her eye toward her ear. She put her hand on top of mine, covering her beating heart.

Completion.

Staring.

The freezing air finds our droplets of sweat and the only solution is to wrap each other tightly. There's no gravity. We're floating in our embrace.

Her face.

She's brushing mine with the back of her fingers.

Completion.

I'm not alone.

Her eyes will blink slower and slower, and this is how we'll fall asleep together.

I'm content.

We can resume when we wake up.

No goal. No script. Moment to moment.

She pulls me on top.

I enter her.

We're intertwined and we're not kissing. Our mouths are locked in, and we use the other's lungs as one breathing unit. We found a rhythm of breathing and exhaling through each other's noses. We're keeping each other alive while creating life. We're thrusting and breathing as one. We're in the NOWHERE and NOWHEN. At times, we violently collide into each other, trying to become one organism through impact.

Dawn approaches.

Her voice is raspy, "Cum for me."

Through making love we astrally bonded. Jacking off to porn was to put me to sleep. I didn't want to just fuck in the forest. I needed to feel the present moment with a real friend. With Luna I felt that for the first time. I release into her. She writhes and pushes against my arms because I'm bruising her from my grip. I release my grip and hug her torso while still wringing out my life force.

I want to die here and transfer into her.

Where am I?

All that exists is Luna.

Anchor, Norm.

I'm in a tent. The sun's coming up. I'm sore where we've rubbed against each other. We're soaking wet and cold from sweat. We give one last quick kiss before we break down the tent and head home.

I like camping.

The sun blinds me as we drive back across the Golden Gate Bridge. We're stuck in stop-and-go traffic with half-awake drivers headed to work in the City. I've never seen bags under my eyes until now. We hold hands the whole drive.

I want to tell Luna that the NOWHERE and NOWHEN and the here and now is what I straddle. Luna, I dread awakening into this. I don't want to be here. I don't want to be alive. Holding your hand reminds me I'm a soul with a body and not a body with a soul. I want to run the clock on this physical existence because I'm a fuck up. I killed that kid. I'm going to die on the streets of Oakland. I don't belong here. Let's run away together.

The California Highway Patrol has stopped the opposite flow of traffic on the Bridge. A line of CHP patrol cars park close to the walkway and railing. There's a suicidal jumper on the outside rail facing the City.

Luna gasps, "Oh my God!"

She buries her head in my shoulder and trembles at the thought that this man could be dead in moments. I press her head into my chest, "Don't look."

She doesn't know she cries for me.

# 13

# HE DOESN'T KNOW HE'S DEAD

## SUMMER 2001

I f you see Cops driving by and think, "They ain't doing shit," you're probably right. Uniformed Patrol can be driving for dollars when nothing's going on. Every now and then, an idiot cop will say, "It sure is quiet." Because of that, a shooting or stabbing will occur during your shift because he said the "Q" word. It's a real thing. Ask a cop. Post hoc ergo propter hoc. After this, therefore caused by this.

Other times, you're taking one report after the other. Chasing paper.

Or, you're shagging calls. Going from one complaint to another.

There's the case of the stolen lawn gnome, the mystery of siphoned gas from a car inside a garage and the best one was from a frazzled cashier at a marijuana dispensary. A customer attempted to use the ATM in their lobby but it was out of cash. The irate customer yelled at the cashier, "Ya'll motherfuckers gon' feel me if I get charged for this shit." The cashier was still trembling even though the customer was gone when I arrived. This nerd from Berzerkley, believing his life was in danger, recounted, "He said I was gonna feel him."

Feel his wrath?

What the fuck do you think he meant?

For clarification, I asked, in my Officer Norman del Rosario voice, "What do you think he meant?"

The cashier harrumphed, "Well, you know…"

No, bitch I don't. Semantics and histrionics aren't crimes.

You called the cops because someone used local colloquialism to express his disappointment at an inoperable ATM. You called because he was Black and loud, and you thought he was going to kill you.

In walks the former angry customer with cash. He's not pissed now because he's about to score a blunt. He sees the smirk on my face and starts laughing. His face reads, "You're here for the angry Black man call." He goes to the same cashier and purchases a brown lunch bag with weed inside. The cashier looks up at me to ensure he's safe.

I waved the customer over to the ATM, showed him the machine's phone number and told him he could just call his bank and monitor that last transaction. "Thanks, boss." We double-take each other, thinking we know each other but don't. Under my breath, I tell him, "You're gonna catch a case for felony feeling emotions." He didn't get it at first. I recap, "Homeboy called and said they were gonna *feel you* if you didn't get your cash."

We both crack up as we spill out onto Telegraph Avenue. Both of us smelled like weed. He didn't have a medical marijuana prescription. He didn't display his California ID card for the weed. Once our feet hit the sidewalk, he was in public, which an easy arrest. Depending on the punk-ass agency you work for, I'd get reprimanded for not pencil fucking this guy. Because we all know exercising the letter of the law creates a peaceful society.

We don't bump fists because ... well, I'm in uniform.

He nods, "See you later."

"Not if I see you first." Right back at him.

He throws up the peace sign above his head as he walks away. This dude couldn't wait. He was hot boxing in his car as I pulled away.

Oakland has real crime. Daily, you'd come across someone who just scored one crack rock. That person who just jay walked with all their weight on their front foot and eyes with focus and purpose just might have a rock. Factoring the time it would take to arrest, transport and process, it wouldn't be worth it because while the world is going to shit with rapes, robberies, shootings and murders you're tied up dealing with just one person who'd tuck under an overpass and smoke. Out of sight. No one rock capers just for a stat. Take the rock, throw it on the ground and grind it into dust with your boots. I've ... heard of that practice.

When you call the police, you reach the Dispatcher. They punch in the details. A man with a gun shooting someone? Where are you? What does he look like? Are there any victims? Or, your car got stolen. From where? Make and model and plate number? The Dispatchers create a call for service, and off you go, fixing the world.

I've been sent to hundreds of homes by Dispatchers. The sight of me in uniform had a spectrum of effects on the nervous systems of those I've contacted. As you can imagine, most were relieved to see me and some despised me.

One home burglary I got dispatched to lingers in me.

I approach the house with heightened concern in my heart before hearing the victim's story. A burglary report writes itself. A piece of shit decides to break into a home with complete disregard for a family's sense of safety and security. That level of violation borders on rape. Feel that in your stomach. Someone's entering your space and then taking your shit without your consent. Top that off with that turd thinking it's okay and you'll get over it. He's making that decision for you.

This report was the same on the surface. Entry point: Back door. Method: Kicked in. Loss: Cash from a drawer in the bedroom. I went to my Patrol car to get my clipboard, but re-entered through the front of the house.

If the old lady who called was Filipino, I'd take her hand to ask for her blessing. Instead, I smiled warmly at her face, moving minimally not to soil her carpet with my dirty boots. Her brow trembles from weakness. She's frail, and her skin is crepey, not only from age. I'm sensing it's from recently releasing a pain she was holding onto. Am I making that up in my head? Am I reading into microexpressions? I'm touched by her smile and I want to cry because she is comforted just because I'm there. I feel ... I see her shoulders drop. She's at ease not from the police. I ease her. She doesn't care about the stolen cash. She only called the police for a report because her son told her to.

There's an indentation on the couch. Someone's favorite spot. Not hers. Someone heavier with a bigger butt. In that spot, something starts to appear. Pick a cloud. Any cloud. Stare at it. Hold your head still. It moves. It morphs. To see the cloud move you can't talk, either. I fixate on this spot on the couch, like staring at a cloud. I stabilize my head and keep my mouth shut. Something that was already there moves slightly and morphs. Imagine a silhouetted treeline or landscape burned into your eyesight from peering into the sun too long near sunset. When you look away, the afterimage projects onto any surface you look at.

This afterimage blob sits in its favorite spot. It's not a two-dimensional cardboard cutout image. I sidestep and see it has a width I can hug. Imagine origami pinwheels made of transparent paper. That's how the surface of this thing behaves—spinning light. I angle my head to catch the light coming from the front window so I can get a better feel for the shape of this spirit and see if I can see any facial features.

"Are you okay?" the old lady caught me staring.

I wasn't only staring. I stood in front of this energy field with my outstretched hand waving back and forth across this invisible space above someone's favorite spot.

I wanted to tell her, this is your husband's seat. I know what he looks like because he's the handsome man beside you in the pictures. His body is buried, but his spirit is hanging out here, but he's disappearing. She knows I know. She just didn't tell me out loud that her husband died last week.

This old lady's son arrived while I was wrapping up my investigation in the living room. I let him know I checked the house to ensure the burglar wasn't still here. I asked the neighbors if they saw anything. A tech is on the way for fingerprints. I added that I'll drive by during my shifts and check on her. I'd want someone to be that thorough for my Mom.

The eldest son shared, "This is the last thing we need."

I nodded because I was tired from talking. Physically fatigued. Speaking takes effort. Like pushing the gas pedal from a full stop. My silence gave him space to empty his thought tank without interruption. He shook his head, "We lost our Dad last week."

"I'm sorry to hear that." In my head, I told him I know what that feels like. I look back at him and flash what my eyes looked like when I cried when my Dad died. He held back his tears.

The police report was finished, and I was grieving with them.

"That was his spot, " he said, referring to the space I was just waving my hands through before he arrived. He pointed to a picture above the couch, "That's him."

I know, dude. This sucks.

I wanted to stay and look into that old lady's eyes. I wanted to warm her hands with mine. Einstein observed energy is neither created nor destroyed. I wanted to let her know her husband's energy is here. I feel him. I see his spirit. I know what he looked like. Half of his DNA is alive in your son, who is here and concerned for you. He's not in the form you want and that's why you're sad. I didn't know him, but he's actually here in memory, in your son and his soul is taking one last lap before he's gone.

When her son went to the other room, she looked at me and flashed a look. "You see him, don't you?" Language isn't the only language. I didn't need to nod to confirm.

I cupped the old lady's hands and handed her the report number.

She tracked my eyes and studied my face because she knew I was withholding one piece of my investigation that I didn't write down. I looked back at her husband's favorite spot.

At that moment, the deceased husband was in full tangible form, as alive as me, the son and his wife. He sat leaning forward with his hands on his knees, looking around like he just woke up from a nap. Despite being an arm's length away from him, he was unaware of me standing in his living room, his wife shaking my hand, his son walking in the other room. He looked like this was just another day, and he was just chillin', oblivious to our presence. No matter how long I stared in his direction, he wouldn't see me.

He doesn't know he's dead yet.

He thinks we're ignoring him, so he's dismissing us.

I look back at the old lady who's seeing me seeing her invisible husband. This time, I don't try to soothe her. I lock eyes with her, and she hears in her head, "You are loved. You had this lovely man for the time that you did. You are safe." At that moment, the stoic sternness and stillness on my face were necessary to deliver that message with clarity. That communication frequency was below that of performing my duty and displaying empathy. THE FACE used that subchannel, I realize.

I left without saying goodbye. She didn't see me walk down the steps with tears in my eyes. Officer Norman del Rosario was tasked with taking a report on behalf of the Oakland Police Department. That report will be entered into the system and a detective will determine that no leads can be followed and then close the case. That will be one more completed call erased from the call for service list, and I will have performed my function.

The past and present overlap. Those spirits still carrying out the same routines are overlapping with the now.

Sit with me, and once in a while, my head will snap to track a wisp behind you. Some ask, "What did you just see?"

"Nothing. Just a fly or something." I rehearsed that response. It explains the identical eye tracking of ghosts, streaking energy orbs or spatial distortions that encircle us.

Once in the shower, before I saw that little white boy kidnapped, I felt a cold spot outside the bathroom door. I stared through the sliding smoked glass shower door at the bathroom door. On the opposite side of the bathroom door, in the hallway, something wanted my attention. I squinted to focus on categorizing it as familiar or unfamiliar. It cloaked itself to look like my Lola. The one who died a year prior to this. In my mind's eye, whatever it was pulled my Lola's image over itself like hiding underneath a blanket. My "not" Lola on the other side of the bathroom door was about to enter the bathroom. "It" used something familiar to get closer to me.

"No." I beam from my eyes. You do not have my consent to approach. Despite the steam of the hot shower, I shivered from the drop in my internal temperature.

Do you think school was my priority? Who can do homework when I'm fighting shit like this off? Throughout childhood, falling asleep, I've heard whispers, "He can see us." What the fuck, man? That's not normal. The attentional resources needed to focus on books and worksheets and lectures were diverted to looking like a student. I moved my eyes from left to right in front of open textbooks, shaded in bubbles on Scantron sheets and sat where I was told to sit. Young children are students. I'll pretend to be one.

One afternoon during school recess, I was part of the stampede exiting the building. The world was blood red. It's like I wore goggles with red lenses suctioned around my eyeballs. Going from indoor fluorescent tube lighting to sunlight took a moment of adjustment. But wiping my eyes didn't reintroduce other colors. The church, my friends' faces, the dry grass field, our blue uniforms remained red.

"Can you see that?"

A classmate said, "You're just hot."

I learned to give only a short explanation. Plus, I didn't

have any words beyond "Everything's red," "The wall's vibrating" or "There are waves around you."

You look with your eyes and you see with your brain. Light bounces off objects, the street, cars, people and enters your eyes at millions of miles per second. Your brain interprets that light. My brain interprets it just like yours. But I have overlapping and simultaneous realities. This world I live in with you. The other one you can't see, but it affects you. I feel your energy signature. Words aren't our first language. It's touch, eye contact, vibrations, soundwaves. Your words are static to me, and I have to really dial in to process the vibrations coming from your throat. There's a delay in my crafting a polite response. But your energy is immediate, and it's not confusing or misdirecting like words.

"Do you see things that other people can't see?" That's an actual question from the intake doctor at a psychiatric facility. The criteria to place someone on an involuntary 5150 Welfare and Institution hold are being a danger to yourself, danger to others, unable to care for yourself and/or non-compliant with psych meds. When the doctor asks that question, I look at the patient because that's a fucking stupid question. We all see things others can't see based on the obvious, let's say, physical positioning. You can't see what's behind you but I can, so yes. I can see things other people can't see. The real question they're asking is, "Do you see things other people would call imaginary?" That's a trap.

One time, Dad took me and my siblings to the park. The drinking fountain button was stuck, and a stream of water leaked, flooding the basin and spilling over the side. I hit Cece on her arm repeatedly to alert Dad to the danger.

Before this life, I died in a flood.

If that fountain doesn't stop it's gonna flood the world and you don't understand human strength cannot resist that current. I flailed, but Cece embraced me to muffle me so Dad could just drive in peace.

Dad had enough and yelled, "Stop!"

He didn't know what to do with me.

No one knows what to do with me, so like a cloaked demon, I wear a uniform. I've learned "Hi, how are you?" back-and-forth scripts. Most importantly, I've learned not to narrate what I see and feel. I'd be locked up in a padded cell if I did. I wouldn't be employable. When I look at you, I see a labyrinth and you're at the center. But your maze is poorly designed. I feel your loneliness that you don't know is there beneath and behind all the stupid shit you do to keep yourself distracted. You know who you are? You're that dead husband in the living room, unaware people long for you.

I haven't constructed an elaborate labyrinth around me. You see, I'm hiding in plain sight. You have so much noise and static that your blind spot is right in front of you.

# 14

## "THE WOUND IS THE PLACE WHERE LIGHT ENTERS YOU"

### SUMMER 2019

My closet is like a sound booth. The pitch black helps it feel like absolute silence. What are those water enclosures called? Deprivation tanks? Like that. I'm cross-legged on the floor. Old suits and police uniforms that don't fit anymore hang on every inch of the garment rod and fixed shelves. Shit I'll never wear again.

I regret becoming a cop. Not only with how it ended, but I'm a square peg for a round hole. An introvert masking as an extrovert for paychecks. When people say they have no regrets and wouldn't change a thing, I call bullshit. There's an inherent self-righteousness that deserves an open hand slap across the face to anyone who confidently and unconsciously says those words. Going back in time with the wisdom and experience you have today and making the exact same choices means you always knew what you were doing with certainty. That's called omniscience which you don't have. If I could go back, I'd be a comic book artist, yoga teacher and monk. Or, if I had the choice never to be born, I wouldn't.

I gave more to my career than it gave to me. I can say that about a lot of things.

I thought I had powered off my phone, but this call came through and the closet exploded with light.

510 area code.

Emiliano.

I pick up, "Am I ass out, fool?"

He laughs his ass off.

We haven't spoken since I got married, moved to L.A. and had my son, who is now a preteen who wants to be dropped off at the mall and left alone. Those aren't the reasons I haven't spoken to Emiliano.

The last time he saw me I was "Grasshopper," a nickname given to me by OG cops because of my Shaolin Monk-like explosiveness and agility. I was also "Skinny Norm" because clothes seem to hang off me. Not everyone gets two nicknames.

When I say I was cross-legged in this closet I lied. My legs are straight out like a stiff action figure. I tell people I suffer from, "rigor mortis." I've kept away from all my Oakland Police family because today, I look like the tired version of Grasshopper who didn't age well.

Emiliano checks in, "You got a minute?"

"For you? 60 seconds." I fire back, keeping things light.

Emiliano clears his throat, "Good. Good. Hey, man. I had a dream."

I trust his intuition and shut the fuck up.

"So, I don't know what this means, but we were on a beach..."

I want to crack a joke like, "Was I wearing pants?" or "Did anyone catch us making out?" But, I could hear he was reluctant to call and wanted to reach me, like, right now.

He continued uninterrupted, "There was this wave that

was about to hit. We knew we could survive it, but we'd be in a spin cycle, maybe dislocate a shoulder but we had antici- pation on our side."

Emiliano and I, together, have what I can describe today as a drone perspective. Add X-ray vision and lie detection. We see around corners. We see intent through people's words and, more so, through the words they withhold from their mouths but speak in their minds. I have my manner of seeing things, and he has his. Our sight synergizes when we connect. With this phone call he's forewarning me of some- thing survivable, but only if I face it head on.

"But, that wasn't it." he adds.

Great.

"There was a wave in the distance. The animals hadn't gone to high ground yet. There was darkness behind that big ass wave. Norm. There was no surviving that one. So, we made the obvious choice, got up and squared up with the smaller wave. As it approached, we both tactically crouched, and you know what? It wasn't shit. We were able to get up and walk off and had enough time to avoid the death wave."

It wasn't shit.

This discomfort of peeling away from a marriage won't last forever. I don't hang out with cops, so resigning doesn't affect my already non-existent social life — not that it ever mattered to me. I must have taken a long beat because he broke the silence with, "How bad am I at storytelling?"

I bust up. Partly because he felt he failed at keeping my attention, which was furthest from the truth. I laugh because I remember a story he told me about when he was in high school and his teacher announced, "Emiliano, you're up." An introvert like me, he hated public speaking. So much so, he avoided preparing for presentations like the one he was scheduled for. We can't get through remembering this story without cracking up. So, he went up in front of the class and was supposed to talk about African indigenous pygmies.

"Norm, the class was spinning. I had to put out my hand on a desk to balance myself."

This is about the time we stop and crack up about how awful we were as students.

He continued, "All I could do was make this shape with my knuckles and say, "Their feet were like this."

This 30-second story, without fail, takes a whole night to recount from beginning to end with laugh tracks.

Emiliano repeats that knuckle thing to his class because that's all he got. An observant classmate announces, "Yeah, you said that already."

Emiliano describes how he's now sweating and needs to put both hands on a desk to stabilize himself. While he's taking deep breaths, he hears, "This nigga didn't study."

His dream, on the other hand, is a visual metaphor for what I was thinking about while he called. In the span of a couple weeks, I was served with divorce papers. I quit my job before they fired me. I put my life on the line every time I put on the uniform. That's a motherfucking fact. And the reason they wanted to fire me was because I told someone who was injured on duty like me, "They don't give a fuck about you."

I was betrayed by the two things I would have given my life for. Here's what I mean. With my life in one hand and the people I swore to protect and serve in the other, I'd sacrifice mine first for the assured survival of the other. I'm the human shield before something harms what's behind me.

This is the smaller wave. I'm getting roughed up. My delusion is the expectation that others will conduct themselves honorably because I did. A lie I crafted and fed into so I could feel like a wanted protector and provider. Emiliano showed me I'm gonna get fucked up, but I'm gonna be alright. And to add, it wasn't that bad.

No, that's bullshit.

It is that bad. I didn't envision being a divorcé, living in a shitty one-bedroom apartment that smells like it has a gas leak. Adding to the humiliation, me quitting law enforcement equals a dishonorable discharge. I'm not authorized to carry a firearm because I'm not considered a retired officer. Retired and resigned are two different things. A dishonorable discharge from a dishonorable department. I quit.

It's the timing of his premonition that was odd. In this closet, this convergence of fucked up bullshit makes the internal chatter incessant -replaying and second-guessing all my life choices. And Emiliano called at the peak of this back and forth in my head.

Like I said, we hadn't talked in probably 15 years and this is the first conversation we have at this exact time? It was time to give him feedback and not leave him hanging. I caught him up with my shame and embarrassment about my failed marriage and ending a career dishonorably. I affirm, "I needed to hear what you told me and I'm glad you reached out, brother."

On the other side of the line he hangs on. I hang on. Holding space for each other.

He breaks the peaceful silence. "Hey, man. I wanted to run something else by you."

"I'm all ears, pimpin'." I don't want this conversation to end.

"Norm. A little while back and what I mean by that is about 25 years ago, you told me about that kid you saw get kidnapped."

I thought I never told anyone. Then I remember I told

him when we first ate tacos together. Emiliano could handle heavy and dark. He was born into that like I was. In fact, that's our baseline. Others lose interest in that level of conversation, but we idle in discomfort. When someone takes an off-ramp, we know they can't handle a dark or supernatural aspect of life. We stay there and stand there in attrition. Whoever is left standing is worthy of our attention.

"I was listening to everything you said, but my crackhead uncle was coming our way."

I remember that.

He continued, "Over the years, I've wondered why you and I hate bad guys so much."

We actually refer to bad guys as bad guys. He paused and was being careful and I could tell.

I relieve him of being polite, "Just say it, man. I need to know what you know."

He explains, "What separates us from other cops is that we're not for the cause for just 40 hours a week. And it's not so much being a cop and upholding the law. It's that look on your face when you told me about not being able to help that kid. You say you froze and you say you were a coward."

I'm forever a coward.

He asks, "How old is your son?"

He's 10.

"So, he's the age you were when you saw that?"

"Yes." I confirm.

"I'd say you did everything in your power to survive. You have to understand, Norm, that your survival instincts had been turned on from growing up in the 'hood coupled with the other shit you perceive. You told me you should've done something. Bang on the window. Yell for your Dad who was hitting the bags at the time it was happening."

I am a Goddamn coward, Emiliano.

I hear him leaning in.

"Look at it this way. With all of your accumulated knowl-edge and martial arts and psychic premonitions, you didn't have that at 10. I saw you holding that 10-year-old to that standard when we were in the police academy, and still, to this day, you're holding that kid to the highest standard life-times above any 10-year-old's capacity to understand those horrible situations."

I'm whipping my 10-year-old self with blades at the end. Cutting him, kicking him, punching him in the head as soon as he shows fear. I've locked this ten-year-old version of myself in the basement to prove I'm tougher than you. I bring him out and punch him in his jaw to show to you if I can do this to myself then you're not shit to me.

"Let me ask you this, Norm. If your son showed fear, ran to you today, what would you do?" Emiliano demanded an answer from me.

My voice cracked. "I'd embrace him."

Right away, Emiliano grabbed me through the phone, "Then why would you punish yourself for being afraid?"

Emiliano locked his grip in me and added, "And let's say you did yell, get your father or whatever. What if he had a gun? In your 10-year-old mind, you didn't say this, but I know you felt it; what if he came back and got you? Self-preservation at 10 isn't cowardice. It's survival."

I'm convulsing with tears.

I accepted what he said next.

"Norm. You didn't do anything wrong."

I can't control my breath.

I die in myself.

I do the impossible and forgive myself.

I'm no longer a cop.

I'm no longer a husband.

But I am a good man.

I'm the best father.

"Norm, I'm so sorry you've been carrying this, but you don't have to."

I kept him on the phone so I don't cry alone.

Emiliano stands guard as I re-open the wound I will now allow to heal properly. He wants me to cry because he knows he's the only one who can protect me at this moment. As Rumi wrote, "The wound is the place where the light enters you."

I nearly nod off when he asks, "You good, man?" knowing he saved me as I saved him decades ago before he was going to get killed by a wanted murderer. I let him go. "Alright, fool. That's enough excitement for one night." He wraps it up with, "Alright, fool. Text me tomorrow."

It is tomorrow. It's the witching hour. I'll text him when I wake up.

I remove the loaded magazine from the gun in my hand.

I lock the slide to the rear, and the chambered bullet flies out.

I catch it.

This was the one that was gonna go through my temple and stop the pain. Emiliano saved me from me and I'll wake up tomorrow, the day after that, and the day after that until God calls me home.

# 15

## USE YOUR WISDOM

### SUMMER 2023

There's an election. There's a war. Someone tell me how shading in bubbles on ballots will right a country and stop people from pulling triggers. Has it ever? Someone tell me how debates and arguments alter the course of self-destruction or unite people. How do advertisements and signs on lawns deepen our understanding of our origins, existence and purpose? I haven't made that connection and am genuinely confused when accosted for my position on a candidate and proposed bill. "I don't know" isn't only an unacceptable answer; I created a vacuum for a diatribe of political or religious righteousness. I'm open to being wrong on this. But I'm right about this; the last words spoken by someone on their deathbed will never be, "I'm glad I voted the way I did."

I've nodded my way through life at people speaking at me or in my direction. Not only have I feigned ignorance about politics, bitcoin and artificial intelligence — I am ignorant. The combination of those words have never been typed in my search bar. From a bird's eye view, we're all stuck in traffic to and from work for decades. We'll try to take tests to get a percentage more above our base salary, and we'll try to secure a long-term sex partner. Then we'll have kids, not for primal evolutionary reasons, but we think we'd make good-looking kids and believe our last names are unique and royal enough to perpetuate. No one thinks that about you but you.

And now that I don't punch a clock for a paycheck but make enough for Target toilet paper pickups, and I'm lone wolfing this phase of life, I get to, what do they say? "Do me."

I live in the desert now. The first night I moved into my house, I jolted from my bed, and my then-partner flinched and screamed, "What's wrong!?"

"It's nothing." No gunshots, no police or news helicopters, no speeding then crashing vehicles, no arguments followed by slaps, punches or people getting pushed over garbage cans or sirens converging onto a crime scene. Nothing.

My soundtrack growing up in San Francisco and working in Oakland were all those ceaseless noises driven by predators attacking prey. I suffered from headaches, but Emiliano had bad migraines later in life. Having your head on a swivel your whole life will create that wear and tear on your neck. A life of constant heightened vigilance had its place. I'm figuring out I can still be aware but not constantly karate chopping someone in the neck in my mind.

My neighbors today have burnt patchy lawns and, intermittently, you'll see a lifted truck with adult human-sized tires breaking the speed limit with the American Flag waving proudly. I went from Oaktown to Awesometown, which boasts it's one of the safest cities in California. I'm looking for, anticipating and am ready to deal with the armed robber and crazy dude with a knife that, statistically, in this place is infinitely less likely to occur. Still. I ain't slippin', fool.

I resigned from the Oakland Police Department and moved down to Southern California to start a family. The relationship went well until it didn't. When things fall apart, the initial strategy to regain footing is to machine gun blame until the other person is humiliated. A never-ending game of back and forth, with each attack increasing in venom and animosity. I'm down for that searing heat of combat and my secret weapon is toeing the line despite pain or fatigue. If pain is your off ramp, I won. Because, Fuck you.

But the ending of a season isn't cause for retaliation. Life trajectories diverging from temporary shared paths is the rule not the exception. Poets and sages likened marriage to pillars in a church. Close but not leaning on each other for support. Instead, they are upholding the same ideals. Who can maintain that stamina when ideals and priorities change? A central tenet the Buddha taught was impermanence. All things change. Or ... shit happens. Love lasts moments to decades but never forever. How can the finite perceive the infinite? Who can maintain a vigilant focus on one's own vision and direction, let alone stand by and hope a lover's gaze aligns?

It is what it is, man.

The ending of the relationship wasn't enough, so life said, "Try this on for size," and I fell off a ladder at my new job and dislodged a vertebrae. I felt like I was stabbed above my ass with every step and pissed on myself throughout the day, leaving that dark pee circle on my crotch with that faint funky odor of drunks at bus stops. Oh, and my dick didn't get hard for months. Work said I was faking my injury, but the MRI, urologist and the supervisor I nearly fell on said differently.

I went off grid.

Or, did my phone just not ring?

I'm alone now.

I read books.

I hike.

I write.

This mundanity is my prayer answered, a reprieve from a world that's always been dialed to 10. I wanted to be alone in peace and "Ta-dah!"

Did you know that on a vinyl record, the lines you see are actually one long, single spiral groove? The needle embeds in that groove and reads the encoded, baked-in music on the black disc. All that music, each individual song, exists all at once — past, present and future.

We are that needle, that contact point in this existence while traveling on individual timelines, moment by moment, on our own records and interpreting the world as we move forward in time. God, Omniscient Consciousness, Allah, Atman, the Universe see your life as a whole, whereas we only have contact with this moment. In these finite and ever-expiring bodies, we tumble forward through time, predicting poorly what the future could be but grasping at the safe script everyone else holds with devotion. We're all doing this thing at the same time, so I don't feel alone, even if the sense of structure is man-made. We're being herded, but to what end?

The harder I avoided the rat race, the more typical I've become. That commoner checklist of high school, college, jobs, career, experiencing too much month at the end of paychecks, marriage, kids and divorce. It's your checklist, too.

Reading the Stoics, Jung, esoteric religious thought and the like and acquiring the ability to paraphrase higher thought didn't shield me from the inevitability of acting out predictable behavior. From the outside looking in that's what I've been. Nothing special.

Or is that the old habit of making myself small to humble myself?

Having sight beyond this present moment, being able to see moments ahead and beyond my present location has been awkward like facial eczema. After all these years, Emiliano has this ability and more and that's it. We have comfort knowing we suffer from this. In that, I'll never be alone. Despite the horrors and levels of existence my brain can't interpret, seeing weird shit differentiates me. In that I am grateful. The source of this uncontrollable fright is the gateway to the beyond and afterlife.

Now, I square up, feet, knees, shoulders and hips toward what I'm shown and others can't see. I am no longer afraid to see or remember.

Remembering. As I hung over the side of my bed, crying myself to sleep after Dad died, that transparent toddler running by that stopped and laughed was his spirit shrugging at me, saying, "What are you worried about? I'm moving on. And playing. You should, too."

I was devoid of compassion for his illness and pain and remembered that Emiliano would tell me I didn't have the maturity to know I was afraid he was going to die and that's how it came out. In penance, I dug my nails in my face and tears, "Dad, I'm a fucking asshole. I HATE myself for belittling you. Accusing you of being weak and better off dead."

Remembering. In the following moment, awake and sitting on my bed, I'm not me as a weathered adult. I'm a child waist high to Dad. He applies a wet, warm towel to my head and combs my hair as he did every morning before school. The teeth of the comb massage my scalp as he meticulously parts my hair, shaping it into an old-school crew cut. The warm water drips down my cheek and I cry louder, "I'm sorry!" I'm a man and child.

Dad combs my hair.

His hand glides to get that precise, clean look.

My crying is inconsequential and ignored.

Dad loves me and knew I would come to this realization.

Remembering. The last time he visited me after he died was before Emiliano saved me. During a bout of sleep paralysis, I was floating through North Beach. Dad leaned up against a pole, smoking a Lucky Strike. I was waking up and losing contact with him. I rapid-fired, "What do I do? Guide me! What am I doing wrong? Who can help me? What do I do about work?" hoping to get a course correction on being lost. Ever since I shunned seeing entities, the beacon on the horizon disappeared and my only course for direction was to continue to check boxes of showing up to work, paying bills and driving the grid. With Dad on the other side, he saw traps, allies and enemies in my life. There's nothing in the rule book that says I can't ask what lies ahead and what to do.

As I walked up to him, he remained facing away having just struck a match and lit up a Lucky Strike. I approached him from his side like a desperate panhandler asking for money. Under his breath, Dad mumbled, "Use your wisdom," and then I woke up.

Wisdom is not a regurgitation of other people's original thoughts. So he was telling me to be quiet and go deeper into myself. Basically, "Shut the fuck up and the answers will come to you." I have access to wisdom.

Even after all this new age study, yoga, what I've seen in my law enforcement career, losing friends to suicide and combat gunfire, I felt I had accumulated enough perspective to understand me. I've seen shit. I must know shit.

During one waking premonition, I walked toward my grandparents who have been in the afterlife nearly my whole life. This time, Lolo and Lola play checkers at the kitchen table. Again, I was a child with my head high as the table. I respectfully walked up to them. Lolo didn't acknowledge me. He remained focused on his game, but Lolo told Lola, "He doesn't know who he is yet." I heard that, Lolo. I'm standing right here. I know who I am. I think. I know my name and my profession; people know my name and stop and recognize me. I'm Norman del Rosario.

Saying my name doesn't tell me who I am.

# 16

## VIP LOUNGE

### TODAY

Set the oven to broil high for about 10 minutes before popping in a frozen pizza. Then, after it's on the rack, set it to 400 degrees Fahrenheit. That'll melt the ice flakes off the top right away and crisp it up just nicely.

My son is upstairs with his friend in the big TV room. They're watching some horror flick, but I sure do hear a lot of jumping in place, singing and laughing. French fries are in the air fryer and two chocolate lava cakes thaw on the counter.

Before they entered the room I told his friend, "When a spill happens. I. Don't. Care." The girl is intimidated by my direct eye contact. She's gonna turn away so I have to send this last message before they disappear, "You have free reign of the pantry if you want a snack. You're VIP. Do not ask. I expect you to help yourself." A sweet and barely audible "thank you" leaks from her mouth.

Whenever my son asks, "Can I hang out with An-"

"Yes." I interject.

Other times he'll start with, "My friends and I were think-"

"Yes!"

Most Preteens and Screenagers will leapfrog over this time without being face-to-face and learning the rhythm of conversation, reading the shift in moods in another's face, and sharing interests in the same niche cartoons.

This innocent time will never return. I want him to savor play because we know what happens after middle and high school.

I lay napkins and forks on a serving tray. I time the pizza, fries and cake so the oven and air fryer alarms go off at the same time. With the tray of steaming food in my hand, I knock on the VIP lounge door with my forehead.

Retired cop life.

Uber. Concierge. Chef. Butler. Security.

On school nights, I make him stand and watch me lay out the pans for his bacon and pancake. I stage the pancake mix box next to the semi-sweet chocolate chips and syrup. I form a small bowl shape with aluminum foil to drain the bacon fat. I lay out the plates, one with a paper towel to wrap the bacon. I take out a fork and grab a cup.

A father's job is to prepare his son for a world where he's no longer in.

My days as an Oakland Police Academy Drill Instructor taught me how to teach. First, demonstrate the skill. Great teachers told me, "Watch me." Lectures, if any, were short. For a kinesthetic learner, I got it.

My son awakens to the smell of bacon. I'm happy to take him to school, happy to pick him up and will drop what I'm doing when he says, "Dad, wanna see this drawing I made?" There is no question as to my expectations when he commits to work, art or any endeavor he shows interest in. Children need presence more than presents.

My Lolo on Dad's side was captured along with American POW's during the Japanese-American war. The Rose Bowl stadium in Pasadena, California would house the amount of American and Filipino soldiers forced to walk to the incarceration camp. Prisoners who fell behind were beaten, bayoneted or beheaded. Dad tapped his head and told my older brother, "He wasn't there when he got back." Dad didn't follow up with, "Be tough." Putting one foot in front of the other in heat, rain, illness and abuse is the minimum standard of behavior.

So, being a cop all those years, driving to work before my son woke up and coming home when he was about to go to bed was normal. It was a privilege. No enemy soldier hovered their bayonet over my head when I was tired. I got it good. I just had to keep on keepin' on.

In early boxing, the referee would chalk a line between two pugilists. The fight would continue as long as the fighters could place their front foot on the line. There were no maximum or minimum rounds. Toe the line. To the death. This was the minimum standard of behavior. With your mouth shut.

I've got one super power in life. Toeing the line. As a cop, I Facetimed my son from the streets, telling him Merry Christmas, Happy Thanksgiving and Happy New year when he woke up. Commitment means sacrifice. Show up to work so I could afford Chick-fil-A parking lot picnics and Lego Ninjago figures.

Today, from the top of the stairs, he summons, "Dad!"

From the bottom of the stairs, "Yes, Anák?"

"Can we get some ice-"

"Yesssss." I cut him off.

He puckers his lips and blows a kiss.

His lips protrude like mine. His eye shape is like mine, but not as "chinito." I am fascinated with this boy. He didn't inherit my eczema. And thank the Lord he's smart. I thank God he's not like me. He's been the top student in his class every year. He's a head-turner. He's been modeling since he was an infant. He's an actor. I want to be him when I grow up.

As he and his friend do what I can only describe as running in a frenzy of circles based on the noise while claiming to watch a movie, I stand guard downstairs. For the soul who wishes them harm, I have premeditated their death. Any person with a molecule of ill intent in their heart needs only to touch my doorknob to unleash the demonic techniques I have trained to deliver. I will toe the line, put one foot in front of the other and throw left hooks until the threat disappears.

The other day, he approached me with his laptop, cueing up a song. "Wanna hear something I came up with?" You know my answer. He pressed play, and a melody arose, followed by a beat, horns and strings.

"I'm feeling an epic fight scene," is my feedback.

"That's what I was going for," he responds while moving the cursor to click and drag and adjust the duration of an instrument.

I test him. "What's the from?" Cartoons from Youtube or TV have catchy intros. I know most of them. I still watch cartoons.

He closes his laptop, "What do you mean?"

"Where did you take that melody from?"

"I came up with it myself."

I've created a space where my son can fall into his own

creativity, play and produce songs from his spirit. Hmm. I'm doing something right.

About the ice cream ... he delivers the news to his friend and "Woohoos" follow.

I pause at the bottom of the stairs, looking up at his after-image of where he just stood. I am today, the Guardian, Under-stander, Destroyer, Hugger and Video Game partner I needed when my path splintered after that little white boy died.

My son and his friend run down the steps, forgetting to bring their garbage down. The joy and untroubled relax-ation on my son's face is what we all strive to return to—that state of mind that was our factory setting before we were indoctrinated to achieve, buy and accomplish.

I remember holding him in my palms when he was a newborn. I paced in a circle in the kitchen when CONVER-GENCE occurred. Nose to his miniature nose. Wrapped like a burrito. He's sleeping, and I bounce and step. Bounce and step. He has a baby booger in his nose, and it's whistling every time he exhales.

From my heart, I beam to him through my fixed gaze, "In my presence, nothing will harm you. I will give you all the knowledge I needed but suffered for. Trust me. I am your shield. You are perfect. I AM you. I love you as I should have loved myself. We are each other. While you ARE me, you are entirely new. The world will lie to you, but I won't." As I bounced and stepped, my being harmonized with absolute love frequency. It emitted from my heart and eyes into the most beautiful boy as he slept in my hands.

"I have never seen you look at anything with that much love," said the mother. "I mean, you're not smiling, but I see it in your eyes. You're serious, man."

We shared a rare laugh.

I remember ...

In 1997.

When my body was exhausted and wrung of energy.

When my father died.

When I was numb from overwhelming grief.

When my Mom lost her husband.

When I was an Oakland street cop.

When friends pulled the trigger to end their pain.

When death taunted me.

When veils of illusion were lifted and spirits and demons could no longer hide.

When I decided my death will be by my hands ...

THE FACE started to speak. But that shit fucking scared me. That singular love, the magnitude of the universe from the Big Bang to the present and beyond eternity, was incomprehensible, so I cowered. It was during my darkest moments that I was able to see what had always been there. The gift of sight beyond the visible light spectrum, beyond space time, that was bestowed upon me was granted by an imperceivable intellect above ours. I didn't summon it. You say it's imaginary. I say okay.

THE FACE admonished me. "I love you. I am your shield. Do not be afraid. No harm will come to you. You see darkness because I want you to see it to protect others as I protect you."

I hold this space for you. I'll keep you safe. If danger moves toward you, I'll let you know. Or, I'll take care of it. Sit with me. Speak. See your reflection in my eyes.

# ACKNOWLEDGMENTS

Cil. Sister. Remove you and none of this happens. You're the gangsterest b-bestie I know. With this book, I want to make you proud. I endure because you fight battles for me until I can do so on my own. I love you.

Bodhi. You're the person I've always wanted to become. I'm truly your number one fan in all of your endeavors. Your imagination is off the charts today and will only grow, but you'll never know how much love I have for you in my being.

Christopher Dela Cruz. Like-minded and like-hearted. I've always been right about your talent, vision and intelligence. This is the baseline expectation. You are evolving and becoming a beacon of creativity and inspiration. I am fortunate to be beside you.

Chris Racina, remember that time you almost killed me with laughter? You've blessed me with your friendship, and I am honored to know you. You mean the world to me.

Cynthia Quiles. Thank you for the greatest gift. Your drive and commitment to your career will always be your guiding light.

Theresa Geier. When I was "off grid" for years you were consistently present offering support, friendship and warmth. May God bless you and recognize you for your pure heart. As I told my sister, remove you, and none of this happens.

Irma Grieve. You championed my career on sheer faith in my ability.

Jose Soto. Little brother. You're all heart. I've seen and read about you saving lives. If you didn't spot that elderly man who fell he would have died. You performed one of many acts of heroism and thought nothing of it. Let's keep laughing and the first to make it to middleweight wins a Filipino food lunch. I know a place.

Julianna Kroncke. Owner of Bespoke Storytelling. You're a God Send. Unleash your superpowers. Take this moment to recognize how you invigorated, shaped and used your whole being to direct this project. Now imagine this multiplied for other aspiring authors and how it can change the Earth's atmosphere.

Gerard Carvajal, who is the toughest of them all? My muse. Your wisdom, patience and love has grounded me all my life. I've always deeply admired the warmth of your spirit. Growing up with you and seeing you now as a father is a joy.

Ed. Older brother. My online swim coach. Your work ethic may comes close to Mom's, and that's immense.

The Oakland Police Department. Too many women and men to mention. Thank you for investing in me to become a leader. (Retired) Police Chief Howard Jordan. You embody, move, speak and decide as the leader I attempt to model myself after.

The Burbank Police Department. Thank you for entrusting me to shape future police officers. I am grateful for the numerous opportunities you have given me to serve in multiple ways.

Jason Bucholz. Author and Editor. Your experience, patience and expertise made me feel safe enough to take my first steps.

David Rose. Editor. I felt your heart and advocacy from across the pond. You gave me confidence in my voice. Thank you.

Ultimately, to Norman the Child. You are one of one. God only printed one of you. Your brain, eyes and spirit were woven to see and feel a little extra because your imagination and creativity could handle it. The difficulties were to make you stronger than you think you could become. Now we meet again. It's safe to play now.

# ABOUT THE AUTHOR

Norman del Rosario is the author of "FLIP," his debut novel. He was born and raised in San Francisco and now lives in Los Angeles. During his career in law enforcement, Norman primarily served as a uniformed Patrol Officer, but also held the roles of Use of Force instructor, certified Crisis Negotiator, Field Training Officer, Drill Instructor and Defensive Tactics instructor. He retired as a Detective. Norman now spends his days creating and writing in coffee shops. "FLIP" is only the beginning. To stay up-to-date on the latest literary works by Norman del Rosario, find him on Substack @normdelrosario.

Made in the USA
Coppell, TX
02 November 2024

39515410R00095